WHITE-ROOMS

DECORATING WITH STYLE, PATTERN AND COLOUR

KAREN McCARTNEY // DAVID HARRISON

PHOTOGRAPHY BY RICHARD POWERS

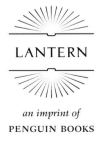

LANTERN

an imprint of
PENGUIN BOOKS

'White...is not a mere absence
of colour; it is a shining and
affirmative thing, as fierce as
red, as definite as black...
God paints in many colours; but
He never paints so gorgeously,
I had almost said so gaudily,
as when He paints in white.'

G. K. Chesterton

CONTENTS

FOREWORD

THIS BOOK CAME ABOUT QUITE BY CHANCE via a collaboration with the photographer Richard Powers on another project. Combing through his impressive archives at his home in Antibes, I was struck by the beauty of the white rooms he had captured over the years and across the globe. It was the decorative range that I was constantly drawn to, in that by not inhibiting any choices, 'white' somehow managed to set the rooms free. Hence a modernist or a Moroccan interior, a Georgian house in London's Spitalfields, a futuristic apartment in São Paulo or a *maison de maître* in France's Lot valley, furnishing white-on-white or with bursts of colour, could all find a place within the great unifying force of white.

'I think of white as a canvas and add layers on top of that. I always paint a room white to gain a spatial sense, a sense of proportion. To me it is the start, even if rarely the finish.'
Sibella Court, interior stylist

There is no doubt that white, combining all the colours of the visible spectrum (as proved by Isaac Newton, I found out) is a dramatic, affirmative choice rather than a passive one. Light reflects, it bounces around and has the effect of lifting the spirits. White has been used for generations, and in many cultures, to symbolise honesty, purity, perfection and spirituality.

It does, additionally, create the sense of a blank canvas, a fresh beginning upon which we can impose our decorative style. Throughout the book you will see examples of how it has been applied: how patterned pastels, bold artworks, antiques, sculpture, designer pieces and found objects all work stylistically within the context of white. Some rooms have impressive architectural features, while others rely on the objects and their curatorial arrangement for their success.

Architecturally, the use of white is widely found, from squat Irish fisherman's cottages with low thatched roofs to the eye-blinkingly beautiful Greek villages, in which white limed walls provide a setting for window frames and doors painted the intense blue of the sky. Not only is white associated with tradition but with modernism: the Bauhaus, with its penchant for basic repetitive shapes, found white enhanced the purity of form and highlighted the absence of decoration. From Le Corbusier to Oscar Niemeyer to Richard Meier, some of the world's greatest architects express themselves most poetically in white.

Yet what is so appealing about white is its great democracy. It doesn't discriminate between high architectural art and a warehouse interior where garage paint can cover every surface, rendering ugly pipes, bricks and stained floorboards invisible. White allows the eye to float over every surface, and it is up to the furnishing, art and objects to take centre stage.

That is not to say choosing the right white is an easy exercise. With literally thousands on the market, it is understandable that certain interior designers have 'go-to' favourites. The orientation of the space matters, as it indicates how much natural light the room gets throughout the day. So, too, does the decorating palette and style. Throughout the book we pull out key points

'Which white to specify is an important decision. As the walls and ceiling are the largest surface area, the choice of white will dramatically impact the interior. Don't underestimate the importance of the choice.'

Fiona Lynch, interior designer

on the factors that make each room work — whether it be textured neutrals against a soft white background, a hint of pink in the paint to tie in with a key decorative feature or the way in which gloss and matt paint contrast. This ensures the book is not only a visually inspiring experience but the deconstruction of each room allows for a greater understanding of why white works in each instance.

There are not only homes with diverse decorating philosophies that illustrate, in depth, the way in which white is the foundation of their style, but sections that cover every area of the house from living rooms to halls and stairways to outdoor rooms. At the back you will find a 'working with white' section with useful advice and tips to start you on a long and beautiful journey with the colour white.

ROSA-VIOLÁN'S INTERIOR IS CONSTANTLY EVOLVING AS OBJECTS ARE PULLED OUT FOR OTHER COMMERCIAL PROJECTS AND NEWLY SOURCED ITEMS ARRIVE TO BE CURATED AND ARRANGED.

1

LÁZARO ROSA-VIOLÁN APARTMENT, BARCELONA

Lázaro Rosa-Violán's home and workspace, in an Art Nouveau building, is testament to his artistic vision. Prototyped furniture sits alongside flamboyant finds and his own art to create a compelling interior with white as its connecting force.

ARTWORKS ARE PERFECTLY POSITIONED IN TERMS OF SCALE AND FORM. ROSA-VIOLÁN'S SKILL IN THE PLACEMENT OF OBJECTS IS ILLUSTRATED BY THE JUXTAPOSITION OF OVER-SCALED STUCCO ROSETTES SITTING BELOW A CHANDELIER, DESIGNED BY PACO RABANNE IN THE SEVENTIES.

'I use white as my catalyst for mixing styles and objects. White acts as a canvas, focusing the eye throughout the entire space, but seamlessly giving it breadth and depth.' *Lázaro Rosa-Violán*

'THE INTERIOR DESIGNER IS AN ACTOR. He must dress up and change roles, understand new identities and integrate them with his own,' says Lázaro Rosa-Violán, a Catalan designer whose distinctive aesthetic is in demand worldwide for restaurant interiors, boutique hotels and retail spaces. An artist by training, he has a strong grasp on the visual world, and his monochromatic artworks make a powerful statement on the walls of the studio. Yet beyond the two-dimensional he knows, intuitively, how to play with scale, with texture and form, and understands how to harmonise decoratively discordant elements. As a self-described 'urban archaeologist', he collects and curates; chairs from the Sixties, a Chinese occasional table, glass-panelled doors from the Ritz Hotel in Barcelona and a chandelier by Paco Rabanne all fall under Rosa-Violán's spell and not only get along nicely but create a new decorative dynamic through their juxtaposition. 'I spend a lot of time studying proportion — of objects, buildings, heights, widths, all controlled elements and how they can blend and complement one another,' he says.

The fact that the building itself is a remarkable space is not lost on Rosa-Violán. 'I love the Barcelona Art Nouveau period, and the original space was an old textile factory. I love to keep the original essence of all my spaces but incorporate my favourite pieces of art, furniture, lighting, even the music, to create a new space.'

The apartment is a majestic shell with high ceilings, white walls, decorative timberwork and characterful parquetry. Rosa-Violán creatively carved up the 200 square metre area, with its circular distribution of rooms, to accommodate personal living space (bedroom, kitchen, guest room and bathroom) as well as communal working areas for his business, Contemporain Studio, and the staff of designers he employs.

While some early 20th century elements remain, such as the oak panelling in the foyer, new spaces were created by using salvaged panels to reconfigure the floor plan to suit a 21st century approach to life and business. The team of skilled craftspeople Rosa-Violán engages on his commercial projects were able to blend the original interior with the found pieces to create a new hybrid that is very much his signature style.

White plays a unifying role as it glides over architectural features that are both simple and detailed, establishing a background for his decorative enthusiasms. The furniture and objects that fill the space, such as a prototype dining table for Contemporain Studio or a button-back leather sofa, generous drapes or crisp bedding, have a common thread. It is white which weaves its way through the decorative heart of this interior. Excitement comes from the wild shifts in scale, exotic provenance, a disregard for era and a sense of style. 'Spaces and the furnishings used to fill the spaces are stories through time, and must evolve and harmoniously come together,' says Rosa-Violán.

AREAS OF CALM BALANCE THOSE OF DECORATIVE INTENSITY. THE GUEST BEDROOM HAS A CUSTOM-DESIGNED BED, AND SITTING BESIDE IT IS A TABLE RECLAIMED FROM THE HOTEL MAMOUNIA, MARRAKECH. A PARTIAL MADAGASCAN FISHING BOAT IS ATTACHED TO THE WALL, SHOWING SOMETHING OF THE SCOPE OF ROSA-VIOLÁN'S SOURCING ABILITIES.

THE KITCHEN IS DOMINATED BY CLASSIC WHITE CABINETRY WHICH, WHILE FORMAL AND
STRUCTURED, IS EASED BY THE ADDITION OF WHITE STORAGE BASKETS. RECLAIMED CABINETS
FORM A WALL OF STORAGE AND AN ELEGANT BLACK LADDER GIVES ACCESS TO A SERIES OF
IMPRESSIVE WHITE BOWLS.

THE APARTMENT'S
ECLECTIC AESTHETIC IS
CONSISTENT, WHETHER
THAT BE IN THE KITCHEN,
WITH ITS IMPRESSIVE
CHINESE SCREEN, OR
MASTER BEDROOM,
WITH ITS INTERESTING
MIX OF ARTWORKS AND
ARTEFACTS SOURCED
FROM DIFFERENT
CENTURIES AND
CONTINENTS. THE
CULTURAL TREASURE
TROVE FROM CHINA,
INDIA AND TURKEY MIXES
WITH A VINTAGE 1970s
LEATHER CHAIR.

LIVING-ROOMS

WHEN IT COMES TO A LIVING SPACE, THE MOST PUBLIC OF ALL THE ROOMS IN THE HOUSE, white is open to hundreds of decorating permutations. In addition, it is often both the largest expanse to decorate and the room that makes the most definitive style statement, creating a degree of pressure in the decision-making process. White as the backdrop plays a significant supporting role to what is placed in front of it, setting the tone of the space.

With its range of furniture pieces and decorative objects, the living room needs a white that works across the design palette of the room. That is why the utmost care is needed when choosing a white — or even a range of whites within the one space. Interior designer Fiona Lynch recommends always using the same wall white on the ceiling. The elimination of the stark contrast between wall, ceiling and floor increases the perceived size of the room and softens the overall look. It is always effective as a means of creating a blank canvas for furniture, art and objects.

In the living space, the 'white out' is a useful, and economical, decorating tool where unsightly architectural features can be made to virtually disappear by painting them white against a white wall. This works either to knock back an ugly, unwanted feature or simply subdue the prominence of a dominant one. Ditto, painting the floor white. This is a popular choice, ranging from the use of solid white to a limed finish to tone down dark or unevenly coloured timbers.

Interior stylist Sibella Court warns of the necessity to look to the context of a living space. 'A leafy reflection of green, a house opposite that is yellow, the brilliance of reflected light from the ocean all affect the appearance of white. I recommend large-format swatching (at least a metre square) and look at it at different times of day.'

While there is something unquestionably calming about white, it can also be used dramatically, in a gallery-style treatment in which the simplicity of white delineates objects within the space. Not everything has to be white, although it can be used to startling effect, as white furnishings within white surroundings create a 3-D flow, as in the case of the living room shown opposite.

overall treatment

MASKING THE DOMINANCE OF KEY
ARCHITECTURAL FEATURES SUCH AS A COLUMN
IS SOMETIMES DESIRABLE. HERE EVERYTHING IS
PAINTED WHITE – EVEN THE FURNITURE IS
WHITE. THIS SPARTAN SPACE WAS GIVEN
TEXTURE AND WARMTH THROUGH RUSTIC
WOODEN TABLES AND ABSTRACT ARTWORKS.

WHILE WHITE DOMINATES ON THE WALLS, THIS ROOM SHOWS HOW SUBDUED
PATTERN CAN WORK IN CONJUNCTION WITH ELABORATE PLASTERWORK.
A SUBTLE ZIGZAG MOTIF EXISTS IN THE HERRINGBONE PARQUETRY AND
IS REPEATED IN THE RUG AS WELL AS IN THE SHAPE OF THE FLOOR LIGHT.

ABOVE DOMINANT PATTERN ON THE FLOOR RUG IS USED AS A FOCAL POINT BUT ALSO EXISTS IN THE CURTAINS TO THE LEFT. CLEAR PERSPEX FURNITURE REDUCES THE INTERRUPTION OF THE RUG'S PATTERN WHILE THE SAARINEN TULIP CHAIR AND LARGE-SCALE ARTWORKS ACT AS FOILS TO THE BUSIER ELEMENTS.

ABOVE RIGHT THE COMBINATION OF THREE DISTINCT ERAS IN THE ONE ROOM WORKS WELL IN THIS INTERIOR. A TRADITIONAL ORNATE CHANDELIER IN BRASS HANGS IN FRONT OF A MID-CENTURY PALE BLUE PAPA BEAR CHAIR BY HANS WEGNER. THE ABSTRACT ARTWORK PROVIDES A SUBTLE COLOUR LINK AND ADDS A MODERN ELEMENT TO THE SPACE.

RIGHT THE TONES FOUND IN THE GIANT ARTWORK IN THIS OPEN-PLAN LOUNGE ARE MIRRORED IN THE MODULAR SOFA AND AREA RUG BELOW IT. THIS SAME COLOUR RELATIONSHIP EXISTS IN THE MOTTLED GREY BRICKWORK, WHILE THE CARAMEL OF THE FLOOR ADDS A NATURAL TOUCH.

A POWERFULLY CONTEMPORARY TAKE ON THE TRADITIONALLY LOW FURNITURE OF THE MIDDLE EAST. A MULTITUDE OF CUSHIONS ADDS COMFORT TO THE SETTING, WHILE AN ABSENCE OF LEGS PROVIDES A GROUNDED SIMPLICITY.

smart combination

SCANDINAVIAN STYLE CAN, UNLESS
USED JUDICIOUSLY, BECOME RATHER
PREDICTABLE. IN THIS INTERIOR,
THE SIMPLE LINES AND TIMBER
FEATURES OF THE DANISH PIECES
ARE JUXTAPOSED WITH STRONG
ANGLES AND EMPHATIC COLOUR –
GOLDEN YELLOW AND TURQUOISE.

THIS PAGE, LEFT THE MIX OF LOW FURNITURE AND A LARGE WALL OF CURTAINS ALLOWS THE CHANDELIER TO TAKE CENTRE STAGE AS A SILHOUETTE. THE DARK TIMBER FLOOR ANCHORS ALL THE WHITE THAT SURROUNDS IT.

THIS PAGE, RIGHT THE GEOMETRIC LINES OF THE ROOM AND STAIRS ARE BROKEN UP BY THE ORGANIC SHAPE OF THE CENTRAL COFFEE TABLE AND SPLASHES OF YELLOW AND PINK.

OPPOSITE PAGE, LEFT STRONGLY INFLUENCED BY THE STYLE OF FILMS SUCH AS *2001: A SPACE ODYSSEY* AND THE FURNITURE OF JOE COLOMBO, THIS APARTMENT USES OVERSCALE PIECES, SUCH AS THE BALL CHAIR BY EERO AARNIO, AGAINST A CLEAN WHITE BACKDROP.

OPPOSITE PAGE, RIGHT A STRONG MIDDLE EASTERN AESTHETIC PERMEATES THIS NARROW LOUNGE AREA WHERE COSY WALL-TO-WALL RUGS AND CUSHIONED FURNITURE ARE LIGHTENED BY TALL EXPANSES OF WHITE WALL AND AN ORNATE MIRROR.

The combination of intricate pattern and large plain expanses
often creates just the right mix of interest and simplicity. Too much
pattern and it becomes frantic and busy, too little and the spaces
risk becoming dull and empty.

WHEN ONE COLOUR IS USED THROUGHOUT AN INTERIOR, A PHENOMENON OCCURS WHERE
LIGHT GIVES THE IMPRESSION OF MINUSCULE COLOUR VARIATIONS. HERE, SHADOWS CAST
WITHIN THE LIVING ROOM PROVIDE AN EVER-CHANGING ARTWORK.

grey area

SOFT GREYS ARE USED IN THIS INTERIOR AS
AN ALTERNATIVE FORM OF WHITE. THE SLIGHT
DIFFERENCES IN GREY SHADES CREATE A SUBTLE
INTERIOR LANDSCAPE. NAOTO FUKASAWA'S PAPILIO
CHAIR AND AN ANTIQUE TIMBER CABINET ARE
UNEXPECTED ELEMENTS IN THE SCHEME.

ABOVE AN ATTIC SPACE IS OFTEN DIFFICULT TO USE DUE TO LOW CEILINGS AND A MULTITUDE OF BEAMS. HERE THESE ISSUES ARE ALLEVIATED BY WHITE PAINT. THE UPHOLSTERED FURNITURE IS KEPT LOW AND PALE WHILE A PAIR OF POUL KJAERHOLM PK22 ARMCHAIRS ADD SOME DELICACY.

ABOVE RIGHT LUSTROUS AND REFLECTIVE FINISHES ARE USED IN THIS LOUNGE ROOM, PROVIDING A SOPHISTICATED LOOK THAT WORKS WELL IN COMBINATION WITH THE EXPOSED CEILING BEAMS. GREY PARQUET FLOORING IS TONALLY CONNECTED TO THE PORTRAIT ON THE WALL AND WORKS TO SUBDUE THE EXTRAORDINARY BOA SOFA FROM EDRA.

RIGHT THE LARGE EXPANSES OF SOFT OFF-WHITE UPHOLSTERY ARE GIVEN A TOUCH OF COMPLEXITY BY GRAPHIC ELEMENTS SUPPLIED BY A ZIGZAG STAIRWAY, A STRIPED FLOOR RUG AND THE SCISSOR LEG ARMCHAIRS. A NEUTRAL COLOUR PALETTE IS CAREFULLY MAINTAINED ACROSS THE FLOOR, CHAIRS AND RUG.

complex geometry

RETAINING MOST OF ITS ORIGINAL
FEATURES, THIS ROOM CAREFULLY
INTEGRATES GEOMETRIC SHAPES IN
THE FORM OF A STARBURST PENDANT,
WARREN PLATNER CHAIRS AND THE
ORIGINAL HERRINGBONE PARQUETRY.
THE RESULT IS FRESH AND EXCITING.

high beam

THE COLOUR AND ANGLE
OF PROMINENT TIMBER BEAMS
ARE MIRRORED IN THE CHOICE
OF FURNITURE IN THIS SUBTLE
BUT COMPLEX INTERIOR. THE
STRONG ARCHITECTURAL
SHAPES FOUND IN THE DAY BED
AND ARCHED SIDE TABLE ARE
COUNTERED BY THE WHIMSY
OF A SUSPENDED BERTOIA
DIAMOND CHAIR SEAT AND
A CONTEMPORARY ARTWORK.

playing with scale

LEFT AN INDUSTRIAL-STYLE SHELL IS AT THE HEART
OF THIS INTERIOR IN WHICH WHITE GLAZED BRICK
TILES AND A STRIPPED PLASTER WALL ARE
SANDWICHED BETWEEN A GLOSS BLACK FLOOR
AND A MATT CEMENT-GREY CEILING. MID-CENTURY
CLASSICS ARE USED ALONG WITH A CONTEMPORARY
SIDE TABLE BY AUTOBAN.

gilt edged retro

RIGHT IN THIS SIXTIES-STYLE IDEA OF A FUTURISTIC
LIVING SPACE, LOW METALLIC TOGO SOFAS BY
MICHEL DUCAROY FOR LIGNE ROSET EXPRESS
A LIBERATED CASUALNESS. RECORD COVERS
AND ANALOG HI-FI EQUIPMENT ARE DISPLAYED
IN A NICHE TO BECOME THE ROOM'S ARTWORKS.

garden party
OPPOSITE EVOKING A CONSERVATORY-STYLE
ENVIRONMENT WITH TROMPE L'OEIL CEILING
AND CURVACEOUS 19TH CENTURY WROUGHT IRON
FURNITURE, THE ROOM USES MUTED SHADES OF
GREEN IN COMBINATION WITH OFF-WHITE TO ADD
A HORTICULTURAL AIR.

gloss over
THIS PAGE SUPERFICIALLY A SIMPLE WHITE BOX,
THE ROOM CONTAINS VISUAL AND TEXTURAL
INTEREST SUPPLIED THROUGH FINISHES. THE END
WALL OF FOLDING GLASS DOORS ALLOWS THE
STRUCTURE TO FRAME THE GARDEN AT ALL TIMES.
DESIGN CLASSICS FROM BERTOIA, AALTO, EAMES
AND CASTIGLIONI FORM A MINI MUSEUM.

ABOVE LEFT A LARGE EXPANSE OF CARAMEL-COLOURED TIMBER FLOORING PROVIDES A SOLID BASE TO WHAT IS OTHERWISE A DELICATE COLLECTION OF WOODEN PANELLING AND GLASS-PANELLED DOORS. THREE DOTS OF COLOUR AND A WHIMSICAL RABBIT SCULPTURE INTRODUCE AN ELEMENT OF SURPRISE.

ABOVE LARGE OPEN-PLAN SPACES CAN BE TRICKY TO DECORATE AS FURNITURE MERGES AND BECOMES VISUALLY MESSY WHEN SEEN FROM A DISTANCE. HERE, THE LOUNGE AREA HAS BEEN DIVIDED OFF WITH A SUSPENDED BOOKCASE, WHILE A HANGING FIREPLACE ALLOWS AN UNINTERRUPTED FLOW TO THE FLOOR.

LEFT THE GRAPHIC QUALITY OF BLACKENED BEAMS AGAINST WHITE IS REITERATED IN THE KENNEDEE SOFA AND CHAIRS BY JEAN-MARIE MASSAUD. THE RUG AND RAW CONCRETE WALLS (FOREGROUND) PROVIDE TEXTURE, WHILE THE ORANGE JASPER MORRISON CHAISE ADDS A BOLT OF COLOUR.

niche area

THE GENEROUS CEILING HEIGHT OF THIS LIVING ROOM
IS FURTHER EMPHASISED BY A LONG LOW NICHE SET
INTO THE WALL AS A DISPLAY AREA FOR ARTWORK,
BOOKS AND OBJECTS. ITS INTERIOR IS LINED WITH
PEBBLES FOR TEXTURAL CONTRAST. THE FINE FRAME
OF THE ARMCHAIRS MIRRORS THE TIMBER SHELF.

culture clash

TRADITIONAL ISLAMIC SIDE TABLES ARE COMBINED
WITH THE SLICK FUTURISM OF THE POLAR SOFA BY
PEARSONLLOYD. THE F3 FLOOR LIGHT BY LUC RAMAEL
FOR PRANDINA CONTINUES THE SPACE-AGE LOOK.
A POLISHED GREY MARBLE FLOOR BRINGS SLICK
AND ARTISAN TOGETHER.

ABOVE IN THIS INTERIOR THE WINDOW AND SOFA CREATE THE SAME LONG, LOW ENVELOPE. BLACK CUSHIONS ARE THROWN INTO THE MIX, PROVIDING A CONTRAST THAT IS SUPPORTED BY THE BLACK LID OF THE DRUM-LIKE SIDETABLE.

ABOVE RIGHT SOFT BUT STRONG, THIS INTERIOR USES CONTEMPORARY VERSIONS OF THE ARCHETYPAL SKIRTED ARMCHAIR FROM THE 1940s. HERE, THE LOOSE COVER IS IN WHITE LINEN. THE GREY TONES IN THE CARPET ACT AS A BRIDGE BETWEEN THE BLACK ARTWORK AND DECORATIVE ELEMENTS TO AVOID A HARSH CONTRAST.

RIGHT WALL-MOUNTED OPEN TIMBER BOXES USED AS SHELVING THROW A HIGHLY SCULPTURAL ELEMENT INTO THE MIX ON THIS LARGE WHITE WALL. THE TIMBER IS THEN PICKED UP IN THE ARMCHAIRS. THE CARAMEL TONES ALSO APPEAR IN THE TIMBER FLOOR, WORKING WELL WITH THE TAUPE GREY SOFA AND ECRU RUG.

green light

KEEPING THE LOUNGE FURNITURE LOW AND LOOSE ALLOWS THIS INTERIOR TO MAXIMISE ITS LEAFY OUTLOOK, GIVING A VIRTUALLY UNINTERRUPTED VIEW OF THE GARDEN. THE SOFA, COVERED WITH CUSHIONS, IS REALLY MORE OF A DAY BED, ADDING TO THE CASUAL ATMOSPHERE.

SOFT WHITE SEATING IN HEAVY LINEN OFFERS AN INSTANT LAIDBACK FEEL,
BUT HERE, THE AREA RUG DICTATES THE MOOD OF THE ROOM AND DRAWS
THE DIVERSE ELEMENTS INTO A COHESIVE WHOLE.

repeating theme
AN ORNATE ISLAMIC-STYLE
CEILING ARCH IS ECHOED
IN THE NICHE ABOVE THE
MANTELPIECE. IN KEEPING
WITH THIS STYLE THE ACCENT
COLOURS ARE EARTHY
ORANGES AND REDS.

ABOVE LEFT THE PINK TONES USED IN THE SOFA UPHOLSTERY ARE A SOFTER EXTENSION OF THE TONES FOUND IN THE FIREPLACE SURROUND. WITH WHITE AND GREY COWHIDES, A FLOKATI RUG AND SHAPELY GLASS PIECES, THE OVERALL LOOK IS ECLECTIC AND FEMININE.

ABOVE IN DISTINCT CONTRAST TO THE GRID-LIKE WINDOWS, THIS LIVING SPACE FEATURES THE UNDULATING LINES OF SIXTIES FURNITURE IN THE FORM OF SEVERAL JOE COLOMBO PIECES AND SOME EXTRAORDINARY UPHOLSTERY ITEMS. THE OPEN-PLAN SPACE IS DIVIDED BY SOFT FLOOR-TO-CEILING DRAPES.

LEFT AN EXTREMELY RUSTIC WOOD STORAGE UNIT IN STONE HAS BEEN TOPPED BY A CONTRASTINGLY PRECISE PLASTERED FIRE SURROUND IN WHITE. THE PINKY TONES OF THE BRICK FLOOR ARE REITERATED IN THE UPHOLSTERY FABRIC CHOSEN FOR THE SOFAS.

THE ENTRANCE TO THE OUTDOOR
SPACE HAS A 'MANAGED' SENSE OF
ARRIVAL IN THE JAPANESE STYLE.
A BLADE WALL ENCLOSES THE
STAIRCASE SO AS TO ONLY REVEAL
THE FULL EXTENT OF THE POOL
AT THE BOTTOM OF THE STAIRS.

2

JOHN ROCHA HOUSE, CAP FERRAT

John Rocha is a fashion, interior and product designer with homes in Dublin and London as well as this one in Cap Ferrat in the South of France. He is a man with a finely tuned aesthetic who knows what he likes and so, he says, all his homes have something of the same timeless feel.

THE VIEW BACK TOWARDS THE HOUSE
SHOWS THE WAY IN WHICH INSIDE
AND OUT CONNECT. IT ALSO SHOWS
THE POWERFUL COMBINATION
OF A LINEAR WHITE BUILDING
WITH A LUSH GREEN SETTING.

'I was very keen to avoid the hip and the now. I did the place more than 10 years ago and I want to still feel the same way about it in another decade.' **John Rocha**

'I COME FROM ASIA AND SO, FOR ME, ASIA IS A PLACE TO HOLIDAY. But given the distance, I wanted to create something with a similar feel, but nearer to my Dublin home,' says designer John Rocha of his French abode. The house he chose was built in the 1950s and had remained in the same family until he bought it in 2003. Attracted by its façade, he was less taken with the small warren of rooms inside. And so while retaining its shell, he set about opening it up, excavating to create more space and a pool and decking area from 'a big patch of garden'. The result is a considered design that cleverly links inside and out by seamlessly merging the two spaces. The two characters of the house live in harmony — the original Fifties villa with its gracious windows and elegant proportions and the spare, linear feel of the newly opened-up rooms and additions. The fact that all spaces, new and old, are white unites the elements, allowing the eye to read it as one entity.

The palette of materials is very restricted — limestone for the floors and kitchen benches, American walnut for the timberwork, and glass — something he is very familiar with from his design projects with Waterford Wedgwood. This simplification of the range of materials was important to Rocha in designing a place that felt timeless — an antidote to the hectic world of fashion with its emphasis on constant change.

It is in the decoration of the house that Rocha's taste for the authentic and handcrafted comes through. He admires, and collects, the work of photographer Peter Beard, who captured images of Africa but treated them in a contemporary way.

This juxtaposition is a defining feature of Rocha's aesthetic. While his own designs furnish the house, he mixes them with chairs from Parisian flea markets, a Kenyan wood sculpture, a lamp from his travels. He enjoys the memories these objects hold and the richness they add to his personal space. Interesting chairs are placed in pairs; he jokes that his children tease him that 'Dad always thinks in pairs.' He admits it's true: 'I don't like singles.'

There is no escaping the remarkable light the house enjoys. Protected by the thousand plants that surround it, including dense bamboo, the white walls and ground of the exterior take on shadow and sun in a painterly fashion. Rocha knows that sunlight boosts his mood; a trip to the house, even in winter, with its blue skies and intense light, can lift the spirit.

As a designer in Ireland, Rocha has not escaped the joys of working with quality linen; a sofa he designed for the house is covered in this practical fabric. 'The sunlight here is very strong and, to me, linen is like a robust old friend, the more you use it the nicer it becomes.'

And there is something of that feeling throughout the house. Objets d'art and furniture have been collected over the years; other items are the result of his long-term collaborations or of his admiration for certain artists or craftspeople. Overall, it is a measured space with considered and curated contents that very clearly mirror the man in the best possible way.

THE HOUSE HAS A QUIET,
MEASURED QUALITY ACHIEVED
THROUGH CLEAN LINES AND THE
USE OF WHITE. WARMTH IS ADDED
THROUGH FABRICS, PAINTINGS AND
FURNITURE, ALL CAREFULLY
PLACED AND DISPLAYED.

ROCHA'S AESTHETIC
REVEALS HIS LOVE OF
ASIA – THE DEEP, DENSE
BAMBOO, THE LOW CASUAL
SEATING AND THE OUTDOOR
FIRE SPEAK OF A SENSE OF
EASE AND RELAXED LIVING.

ROCHA'S PASSION FOR CHAIRS FINDS EXPRESSION INSIDE AND OUT. THE CURVED CANE CHAIRS WITH AN OPEN DESIGN CONTRAST WITH THE SOLIDITY OF THE WHITE WALLS AND THE OTHER MORE STRUCTURED UPHOLSTERY PIECES, AND ALLOW LIGHT TO POUR THROUGH TO CREATE INTERESTING SHADOWS.

SIMPLE TOUCHES PULL THE COLOURS
OF OUTSIDE IN. A BEDSPREAD IN
SHADES OF GREEN AND BLUE AGAINST
CRISP WHITE SHEETS ECHOES THE
EXTERIOR FOLIAGE AND THE COLOURS
OF THE WATER AND POOL SURROUND.

KITCHEN & DINING

USING WHITE IN DINING ROOMS AND KITCHENS IS A TRIED AND TESTED FORMULA, providing a light, fresh space that is extremely easy to add to decoratively. When part of an open-plan environment, it is important to think about the surrounds and how the rooms and functions relate. Tying spaces together through the use of white simplifies the overall scheme and allows individual objects to gain attention without having to compete with distracting changes in colours and finishes, patterns and textures. In this instance, less really is more.

Whether your kitchen and dining room are integrated or separate, the relationship between them demands a complementary treatment. White provides a bridge between the kitchen, an area of almost constant activity, and the dining room, an undeniably calmer part of the house. Think of the rooms as twins; the same but different.

While kitchens need to be practical, it is no excuse for them to be uninspiring. The decorative scope is unlimited, from the rusticity of exposed plumbing and concrete benches to the polished precision of island benches and seamless storage. White can tie all these elements together, and also help to quieten down the busyness of necessary kitchen paraphernalia and provisions.

In the case of the dining room, designer Thomas Hamel believes that white provides the perfect backdrop for art, with the art itself becoming the dominant decorative feature. When using this approach, he wallpapers the room in a slightly textured pure white silk. 'This achieves the most elegant texture, as light reflects, and the rhythm from the seams of the panels is effective,' he says. 'It is extremely subtle, but the sophisticated eye notices the effect.'

Within the purity of white, style is one thing but creating a beautiful dining room requires some thought of practicalities. Pay attention to the relationship between tables and chairs in regard to height, materials, proportion and scale; awkward arrangements rarely look good. Embrace the decorative excitement a well-placed rug or a feature light can provide. What is notable in this chapter is the success of simplicity — a few well-chosen items, confidently placed, works every time.

in the zone

A SLIDING DOOR SET INTO
THE WALL CAVITY CREATES THE
POSSIBILITY OF TWO DISTINCT
ZONES FOR THE LOUNGE AND
DINING AREAS BUT THE TWO
ROOMS ARE CONNECTED BY
THE CONTINUOUS WHITE FLOOR.
THE PLUSH LOUNGE ROOM IS
CONTRASTED BY TALL INDOOR
TREES AND KONSTANTIN GRCIC'S
GRAPHIC CHAIR ONE.

free flow

KEEPING THE STAINLESS STEEL
KITCHEN AS FREESTANDING UNITS ON
LEGS ALLOWS THE PARQUET FLOOR
TO FLOW, VISUALLY INCREASING
THE SIZE OF THE ROOM. THE TIMBER
FLOOR ALSO CONNECTS WITH THE
FLUTED TIMBER ARCHITRAVES.

ABOVE THE ROOM HAS A PREDOMINANTLY UNIFIED APPROACH WITH TRADITIONAL ORNATE PLASTER CEILING, QUEEN ANNE–STYLE CHAIRS AND A TURNED TIMBER FLOOR LIGHT. THE SINGLE SURPRISE ELEMENT IS THE CONTEMPORARY MULTI-ARMED DOUBLE OCTOPUS CHANDELIER FROM TURKISH DESIGNERS AUTOBAN. THE FLOOR LIGHT, KING, IS ANOTHER OF THEIR DESIGNS.

ABOVE RIGHT THIS LONG GALLEY-STYLE KITCHEN IS SUNKEN SO THAT THE BENCHES ARE AN EXTENSION OF THE LOUNGE ROOM FLOOR. THE EYES ARE FORCED TO MOVE FROM THE KITCHEN TO THE LOUNGE AND ULTIMATELY TO THE VERTICAL GARDEN WALL OUTSIDE. THE WHITE INTERIOR AND EMPHASIS ON VIEW SERVE TO OPEN UP THE NARROW SPACE.

RIGHT MAKING THE MOST OF A POTENTIALLY DRAB AREA UNDER THE STAIRS, CUPBOARDS ARE REPLACED WITH GLAZING TO ALLOW LIGHT AND GREENERY INTO THE DINING SPACE. THE STAIR'S VERTICAL SUPPORTS ALSO CREATE A PLEASING 3-D FOCAL POINT.

light and shade

OPPOSITE THE SLIM DARK BENCHTOP DRAWS THE EYE
ALONG THE ROOM TO THE STEEL GRID DOOR AND
CEILING PANELS ABOVE. THE RESTRAINED PALETTE
AND POTENT CONTRAST OF LIGHT AND DARK ARE THE
ELEMENTS THAT MAKE THIS SOLUTION SO POWERFUL.

on the grid

THIS PAGE THE GRID-LIKE WINDOWS AND THE STRIPES
OF THE FLOOR RUG NATURALLY WORK WELL TOGETHER
BUT OPTICAL OVERLOAD IS PREVENTED BY A SIMPLE
CIRCULAR TIMBER TABLE TOP.

THIS PAGE, LEFT WITH ITS SPECTACULAR TIMBER-LINED CEILING
PROVIDING ALL THE CHARACTER THE ROOM REQUIRES, THE UNITS
IN THIS LARGE OPEN KITCHEN CAN REMAIN MINIMAL.

THIS PAGE, RIGHT IN SIMILAR DARK CHOCOLATE TONES, THE TIMBER
TABLE AND TIMBER FLOOR PERFECTLY BALANCE ONE ANOTHER. THE
WALL-HUNG SIDEBOARD ALLOWS THE FLOOR TO CONTINUE RIGHT
TO THE WALL, EXAGGERATING THE ROOM'S SIZE.

OPPOSITE PAGE, LEFT AN EXPANSIVE DOUBLE-HEIGHT SPACE ALLOWS
FOR A LARGE TABLE TO COMPLEMENT RATHER THAN DOMINATE THE
ROOM. THE LINEAR SHAPE ECHOES THE ROOM'S GEOMETRY.

OPPOSITE PAGE, RIGHT A PLAYFUL VARIATION ON TRADITIONAL
DECORATIVE ELEMENTS, THIS DINING AREA COMBINES THE
BURNT FRAMES OF THE SMOKE CHAIR FROM MOOOI, AN
ORNATELY SHAPED WINDOW AND PLASTER PLAQUES.

Contrasting dark timber floors with white walls and ceilings has
a grounding effect while allowing the white to amplify the proportions
of the space. The timber also adds character and prevents the scheme
from becoming too clinical. Timber ceilings achieve a similar effect,
but reduce the perceived height.

graphic content

OPPOSITE A STRONG BLACK AND WHITE GRAPHIC DRAWS
THE EYE AWAY FROM THE LOW CEILING. THIS PROBLEM IS
ALSO ALLEVIATED BY THE SIMPLE TRICK OF PAINTING THE
BEAMS WHITE.

light show

THIS PAGE THIS LARGE CONVERTED WAREHOUSE HAS
A SMALL KITCHEN BUT AN ENORMOUS LOUNGE AND DINING
SPACE. TWO OVERSIZED INDUSTRIAL PENDANTS ARE USED
TO CREATE A MORE INTIMATE ZONE FOR THE DINING AREA.

ABOVE THIS COMPACT KITCHEN USES RECLAIMED TIMBER FOR THE DRAWER FRONTS AND A TYPE OF PINBOARD DEFINED BY A DISTRESSED PICTURE FRAME TO PROVIDE A TOUCH OF BOHEMIAN CHARACTER. THE CUTE CARAVAGGIO PENDANT LIGHTS WITH RED CABLE ARE FROM DANISH BRAND LIGHTYEARS.

ABOVE RIGHT A HIGHLY ORIGINAL SOLUTION TO A KITCHEN SANDWICHED BETWEEN DINING AND LOUNGE SPACES, THIS DESIGN USES A THREE-SIDED BOX OF PYRAMID-SHAPED MODULES TO HIDE THE KITCHEN WORKINGS. MAKING THE WALLS MORE LIKE A ROOM DIVIDER TURNS IT INTO A DECORATIVE STATEMENT.

RIGHT WHILE MAINTAINING THE DECORATIVE QUALITIES OF A PLASTER CEILING ROSE, THE DESIGNER HAS CREATED A KITCHEN WITH MODERN INDUSTRIAL OVERTONES. THE TRIO OF 265 WALL LIGHTS FROM FLOS AND THE METAL BARSTOOLS HAVE A MECHANICAL QUALITY THAT COMPLEMENTS THE CHUNKY TIMBER TABLE TOP.

focal point

THE CHOICE OF A LONG SLIM TABLE ACCENTUATES THE
PROPORTIONS OF THE ROOM AND DRAWS THE EYE
TOWARDS THE FEATURE WINDOW. THE CH24 CHAIRS
BY HANS WEGNER WORK PARTICULARLY WELL WITH
THIS STYLE OF TABLE. THE LIGHT IS THE TARAXACUM
BY ACHILLE CASTIGLIONI FOR FLOS.

ladder proof

THIS PAGE THE SLIDING LADDER SYSTEM ALLOWS ACCESS
TO HIGH STORAGE AND BRINGS A SCULPTURAL ELEMENT TO
THE SPACE. THE HONESTY OF A SOLID TIMBER SLAB TABLE
AND BENCHES PROVIDES A PERFECT FOIL FOR THIS.

opening numbers

OPPOSITE WITH MULTIPLE LARGE OPENINGS TO OTHER ROOMS,
THE KITCHEN FEELS LIGHT, SPACIOUS AND CONNECTED. THE
SIMPLICITY OF THE ISLAND BENCH PROVIDES A DELICIOUS
CONTRAST TO THE INTERESTING ARCH SHAPES.

The complex geometry of a house can be used to great effect, especially if various elements within the scheme are kept deliberately simple and unadorned.

ABOVE LEFT AN OPEN-PLAN LIVING/DINING SPACE IS DIVIDED INTO MORE INTIMATE AREAS BY A LARGE MODERNIST FIREPLACE, MAINTAINING INTERESTING VIEWS BETWEEN THE ROOMS. RUGS ALSO DESIGNATE ZONES IN THE CONTINUOUS WHITE FLOOR.

ABOVE A COMPACT KITCHEN WITHIN PARTITION-LIKE WALLS MAXIMISES SPACE WITH WRAPAROUND SHELVING. PALE BLUE LAMINATE AND STAINLESS STEEL ARE EMPLOYED BUT GROUPINGS OF OBJECTS IN TURQUOISE ADD A DECORATIVE QUALITY AND CONNECT THE KITCHEN TO SURROUNDING ROOMS.

LEFT SLIDING DIVIDING WALLS SEPARATE THE GALLEY KITCHEN FROM THE LOUNGE/DINING AREA. THE SIMPLE ARCHITECTURE LEAVES PLENTY OF SPACE FOR THE OWNER'S COLLECTION OF FORTIES MODERNIST FURNITURE BY FRENCHMAN JEAN PROUVÉ (CHAIRS, TABLE, LOUNGE CHAIR AND WALL LIGHT) AND SHELVING BY CHARLOTTE PERRIAND.

take shape

THIS KITCHEN IS ALL ABOUT SHAPE. SMOOTHLY
SCULPTURED WALLS OFFER A DYNAMIC CONTRAST
TO THE ANGULAR FORMS OF THE CUSTOM-DESIGNED
CENTRAL ISLAND. EVERYTHING ELSE IS SIMPLE AND
HIGHLY CONTROLLED, WITH THE TIMBER FRAMING
OF THE WINDOWS ECHOED IN THE ARTWORKS.

opposites attract

WHAT IS LARGELY A BLANK CANVAS, DUE TO IT ALL BEING PAINTED WHITE, IS TRANSFORMED BY TWO OPPOSING ELEMENTS – ON ONE HAND, THE HIGHLY DECORATIVE STYLE OF A STUDIO JOB PAPER CHANDELIER AND A TRADITIONAL TURNED LEG TABLE; ON THE OTHER, ANGULAR SCISSOR LEG CHAIRS AND A TRIPOD LAMP.

bench mark

LEFT IN THIS LONG NARROW KITCHEN THE OWNERS
HAVE CLEVERLY SAVED SPACE AND REDUCED
CLUTTER BY ELIMINATING A FEW DINING CHAIRS AND
REPLACING THEM WITH A LONG, LOW BANQUETTE
THAT FLOWS DIRECTLY OFF THE END OF THE
KITCHEN BENCH TO FORM AN INTEGRATED UNIT.

gallery kitchen

RIGHT THE EMPHASIS IN THIS AREA IS DEFINITELY
ON THE ART. BY KEEPING THE KITCHEN AS SIMPLE
AS POSSIBLE, IT ALLOWS THE HOUSE TO ACT AS
A GALLERY SPACE WHERE THE FLOOR-TO-CEILING
ARTWORKS CAN REALLY SING. THE OAK FLOOR
ADDS A LITTLE DOMESTICITY TO THE SCHEME.

wood works

THE ROOM EXUDES AN HONEST QUALITY,
AS SOLID TIMBER SHAPES WORK WITH THE
SCULPTURAL FORM OF THE LADDER. EXPOSED
JOISTS ARE SIMPLY WHITEWASHED TO KNOCK
BACK THEIR DOMINANCE.

ABOVE LEFT A ROUND BLACK TABLE MAKES A STRONG VISUAL STATEMENT IN THIS ALL-WHITE DINING ROOM. PHILIPPE STARCK'S TRANSPARENT GHOST CHAIRS FROM KARTELL BECOME ALMOST INVISIBLE, MAKING THE TABLE EVEN MORE OF A FEATURE.

ABOVE A HEFTY BUTCHER'S BLOCK TABLE IS MIRRORED BY A CEILING OF ORIGINAL EXPOSED JOISTS, PAINTED WHITE TO GIVE THE IMPRESSION OF A TALLER SPACE. THE SILVERY GREY OF THE TIMBER PARQUET FLOOR FINDS THE PERFECT MATCH IN VINTAGE METAL-FRAMED CHAIRS.

LEFT THIS NARROW GALLEY-STYLE KITCHEN IS OPEN ON ONE SIDE WITH A MIRRORED SPLASHBACK TO BOOST THE IMAGE OF LIGHT AND SPACE. THE KITCHEN TABLE SITS SNUGLY BENEATH OVERHEAD CUPBOARDS WHILE A SLIT WINDOW ADDS A VERTICAL ELEMENT TO THE SPACE.

3

ERICA TANOV HOUSE, BERKELEY

For designer Erica Tanov, decorating is an emotional and intuitive business. The pieces in her home, sourced from travels, auctions and eBay, sit alongside her own designs – all showcased within the context of a calming white interior.

TANOV FOUND AREAS IN THE
HOUSE WHERE SHE CHOSE TO
LEAVE THE LAYERS OF PEELING
PAINT UNTOUCHED, ALLOWING
THE VISIBLE HISTORY OF THE
HOUSE TO CONTRIBUTE TO ITS
PRESENT DECORATIVE SCHEME.

'I'm always bringing a bit of nature inside, whether it's flowers from our garden or bits and pieces of twigs, leaves, feathers; anything, really, that intrigues me. These are the things that provide the most inspiration in my design process.' Erica Tanov

IT IS IMPOSSIBLE NOT TO BE DRAWN INTO THE CHARM OF DESIGNER Erica Tanov's visual world as she seems to imbue everything she touches with a seductive sense of ease. She was trained at Parsons School of Design in New York as a fashion designer but, since her move back to California, has spread her creative wings to include homewares – bedding, candles and furniture – with a broader offering on the way. Her distinctive aesthetic is present in every part of her business but is at its most joyful and intense in the home she shares with her husband, musician Steven Emerson, and two children Isabelle and Hugo. When asked to sum up her home, in essence, she is unequivocal. 'Relaxed, comfortable, refined hippie, lived-in grandeur,' she says.

Finding the perfect house was a case of serendipity. A colleague mentioned that her grandfather was getting ready to sell his place. 'It was on a street I had long loved so I rushed to go see it before he put it on the market,' says Tanov. 'It needed work but the light was so beautiful throughout. I was looking for a diamond in the rough, as this indeed was.'

Situated in Berkeley, the connection to nature is profound. 'My home studio (which we call the tree house) is surrounded by oak trees, providing me with endless inspiration and peace of mind. I love gardening – hands in the dirt, pulling weeds, tending plants, witnessing new miraculous growth. It's very grounding for me, being in the present moment.'

Having an architect father, Tanov has 'always been drawn to interior spaces and creating beautiful surroundings'. In approaching the interior of her rough diamond of a house, she says that 'while retaining the original floor plan, we focused on maintaining the integrity of the house and restoring it to its original state'. This involved tearing out some of the less than desirable lighting treatments and built-in cupboards that had been installed in the Seventies and Eighties. 'The rest was primarily cosmetic – painting (mostly white); wallpapering; installing long-collected light fixtures and filling the place with treasured pieces,' says Tanov.

Tanov's decorating approach is intuitive and expansive. Never limiting herself to one specific era, period or style, she artfully combines what she loves. 'I'm drawn to things with history and a kind of raw beauty. Each piece, whether it's collected from a trip or found at a flea market has some kind of meaning to me,' she says. Indeed, it is the context of white that gives the necessary background to her idiosyncratic mix of estate sale finds, family heirlooms and objects that cross cultural boundaries. 'White works as a perfect canvas for adding elements of colour and texture,' says Tanov. 'It's completely versatile and I never tire of it. White feels clean and clears the mind. I find it extremely soothing.'

Predominantly the feeling is of a home that is comfortable and lived-in. Books are not colour-coded, nor are images that appeal to her framed but, instead, are torn out of magazines and stuck to the wall. There is a genuinely impromptu energy that is about instinctive placement and ease of being. It is an interior that has accrued over the years with thought and love, and it shows.

IT'S ALL ABOUT
PLACEMENT –
THE NATURE OF THE
BOOKSHELVES WITH
THEIR HIGGLEDY-
PIGGLEDY CONTENTS
AND COLOURS ARE
A BACKDROP TO THE
SIMPLE LINEAR FORM
OF A WHITE MID-
CENTURY CHAIR AND
A CARVED MANGO
WOOD STOOL BY
ERICA TANOV.

TANOV'S FAVOURITE WHITES INCLUDE BENJAMIN MOORE SUPER WHITE AND FARROW & BALL POINTING. THE SHELVING SHOWCASES A SOFTLY TONED MIX-AND-MATCH COLLECTION WITH BLUE, PINK AND GREEN AS HIGHLIGHTS. A SIMPLE DIAPHANOUS CURTAIN IS PULLED BACK TO REVEAL A GROUPING OF GLASS VESSELS.

SO MUCH OF TANOV'S APPROACH IS
SUMMED UP IN THIS ONE IMAGE – THE
OPULENT BUT PLEASINGLY FADED
WALLPAPER BY DE GOURNAY, HER
OWN BEDDING DESIGNS DRAPED IN A
MOROCCAN WEDDING BLANKET AND
A 1960s CREDENZA FOUND AT A MARKET.

BEDROOMS

THE IDEAL BEDROOM IMPARTS A FEELING OF RESTFULNESS AND CALM. It helps promote sleep and offers a life-affirming place to wake up each morning. Outside of these broad goals, however, a successful decorating scheme can be created in many different ways. As much as white is a symbol of cleanliness in bathrooms and kitchens, it promotes the idea of softness in bedrooms – think white goose feathers, pillows and eiderdowns. White in this environment has a cocooning effect. It is no accident that hotels promote their luxury credentials with crisp bed linen.

White walls reflect morning light, ensuring a bedroom is uplifting enough to provide a fresh start to each day. Bedrooms often benefit from the ability of white to make a room appear larger; architectural features such as ceiling beams or distracting detailing can be painted out to elevate the perceived height, and floors whitened to merge with the walls. Often, interior designers, aware that as the largest surface area in a home, the choice of wall colour will dramatically impact the interior, steer clear of whites with a tinge of yellow, preferring the palest of pinks as a more flattering option. They recommend a grey-toned white for a moodier feel, a natural, fresh white for all-purpose decorating, and to paint the walls and ceiling in the same white. Softer whites are forgiving and carry hidden complexities in their near imperceptible tints, transforming under different lighting conditions.

Decoratively, a white-painted interior offers some quiet areas on which it is possible to build layers of pattern, place reflecting mirrors, coloured artwork, graphic lighting or walls of books.

White in a bedroom lends itself to the subtle layering of shades in bedclothes, cushions and soft furnishings, adding to an all-round feeling of tranquil comfort.

Used in bedrooms for privacy and light control, curtains afford another opportunity for decorative interest. White fabrics work particularly well, folding to create soft shadows that not only enhance the textural qualities of the material but often give a pleasing diffused light.

These pages take you on a journey of the way in which white provides a clean slate for simple statement pieces, a play of pattern or significant shots of colour.

whiter shades

THE SOFT, ROUNDED SHAPES OF THE FLASH
TABLE LIGHT FROM OLUCE, ALESSI ASHTRAY AND
PLASTIC STORAGE UNIT HAVE A STRONG SIXTIES
FEEL. TO AVOID THE VARIOUS SHADES OF WHITE
AND IVORY BECOMING MURKY, THE OWNER HAS
ADDED CRISP WHITE SHEETS AND PILLOWCASES.

reflective factor

DECORATIVE ETCHED MIRRORS, MIRRORED FURNITURE
AND A CRYSTAL CHANDELIER UNDERLINE AND REFLECT
THE GENEROUS PROPORTIONS OF THE ROOM.
EVERYTHING, RIGHT DOWN TO THE FINE METAL-FRAMED
DAY BED, ENSURES THE ROOM STAYS LIGHT AND BRIGHT.

 ABOVE USING TRADITIONAL MATERIALS SUCH AS PORCELAIN OR GLASS ABOVE THE BED, AS SEEN HERE IN THE WALL-MOUNTED BONE CHINA LIGHT FITTINGS BY BRITISH COMPANY BTC, BREAKS UP THE WALL SURFACE AND PROVIDES A DOSE OF OLD-WORLD CHARM. THE USE OF VERTICAL LINES AND A SYMMETRICAL PLACEMENT GIVES A SIMPLIFIED DECO FEEL.

ABOVE RIGHT CLEAN CONTEMPORARY ARCHITECTURE REGULARLY FEATURES FLOOR-TO-CEILING GLASS FOR A SEAMLESS CONNECTION TO THE OUTSIDE, BUT THIS CAN APPEAR A LITTLE COLD AND CLINICAL AT TIMES. HERE THE OWNERS HAVE ADDED FULL-LENGTH DRAPES TO SOFTEN THE RIGID LINES AND ADD PRIVACY.

 RIGHT IN A ROOM WITH IDIOSYNCRATIC FEATURES – STAIRS BREAKING THE CEILING LINE AND WIDE OLD FLOORBOARDS WITH OBVIOUS GAPS – THE OWNER HAS CHOSEN TO UNIFY THE ELEMENTS BY PAINTING EVERYTHING IN A SHADE OF WHITE. AN OLD-FASHIONED BED CONTRASTS WITH A LIGHT BY PHILIPPE STARCK.

shelf life

OPPOSITE IN ROOMS WHERE THERE IS NO ESCAPE FROM THE SQUARE OR RECTANGLE, A BOOKSHELF FILLED WITH RANDOMLY PLACED BOOKS CAN BE A HIGHLY ARTISTIC BUT CONTROLLED FORM OF CHAOS, SUPPLYING VARIABLE SIZE AND COLOUR.

organic chemistry

THIS PAGE AS AN ANTIDOTE TO THE HOMOGENEITY OF JUST WHITE, BLACK AND WHITE WALL DECALS AND WALLPAPERS OFFER AN INJECTION OF GRAPHIC SIMPLICITY OR ORGANIC LYRICISM, AS SEEN IN THE OUTLINE OF A LIFE-SIZE TREE.

THIS PAGE, LEFT THE SURPRISE OF A TEXTURED WALL SURFACE
IN THE FORM OF FULL-LENGTH CURTAINS ELEVATES THE BEDROOM
TO A NEW LEVEL OF SOPHISTICATION.

THIS PAGE, RIGHT RICH TIMBER IN CHOCOLATE TONES, AND WITH
OBVIOUS GRAIN, CONTRASTS SPECTACULARLY WITH THE SIMPLICITY
OF WHITE PAINTED WALLS AND CLEAN, WHITE LINEN.

OPPOSITE PAGE, LEFT A SPARTAN WHITE LOFT WITH MONASTIC
OVERTONES IS TRANSFORMED INTO A CONTEMPORARY MELTING
POT BY CASUALLY PROPPED LARGE-SCALE ARTWORK AND ACID
GREEN CANDELABRA.

OPPOSITE PAGE, RIGHT IN CONTRAST TO THE WALLS OF NARROW
PAINTED TIMBER BOARDS, THIS BEDROOM INCORPORATES AN
IMPACTFUL SIXTIES LAMP FITTING IN TIMBER AND MILK WHITE GLASS.

Keeping bedrooms devoid of clutter provides a relaxing haven from the hectic business of daily life. Just a few select pieces are required to add interest to an otherwise clean and peaceful space.

calming influence

THIS PAGE WHITE IS THE PERFECT BACKDROP TO INTENSE PATTERN. HERE IT ENABLES AN ECLECTIC MIX OF BLACK AND WHITE TILES, FOIL WALLPAPER AND DECORATIVE PANELLING TO COLLIDE HEAD-ON IN THE ONE ROOM.

by contrast

OPPOSITE THE NATURAL CONTRAST TO WHITE IS, OF COURSE, BLACK. THE OWNER HAS USED FINE CONVERGING BLACK LINES (JUST LIKE ON THE LIGHT FITTING) IN THE CORNERS OF THE CEILING TO ACCENTUATE ITS SHAPE AND HEIGHT.

ABOVE THIS WHITE ROOM USES MINIMAL LINES OF COLOUR AS A RESTRAINED HIGHLIGHT. THE HORIZONTAL LINES OF GOLD ON THE ALVAR AALTO BEEHIVE LAMP AND THE DELICATE ZIGZAG PATTERNS IN THE QUILT ADD SUBTLE LAYERS TO THE INTERIOR, AS DOES TOM DIXON'S OFFCUT STOOL.

ABOVE RIGHT THE CRISP WHITE FORMALITY OF THE FIREPLACE SURROUND AND PANELLING IN THE BEDROOM IS SUBTLY DIFFUSED BY THE USE OF THE PALEST OF BLUE HUES ON THE WALLS AND BUILT-IN WARDROBE. A FORNASETTI VASE ADDS A MORE INTENSE TOUCH OF THE SAME COLOUR.

RIGHT WHITE BECOMES A HIGHLIGHT WHEN USED IN CONTRAST TO A FEMININE PALETTE OF SOFT PASTELS, AS SEEN HERE IN PALE BLUES, LICHEN GREEN AND MAUVE. THE BUILT-IN WARDROBE IS MADE MORE PRECISE AND MORE COMPLEX BY CLEAN WHITE TRIM.

tone poem

TONAL GREYS AND TAUPES COMBINE
BEAUTIFULLY WITH WHITE WITHOUT CREATING
A STRONG CONTRAST. THE GREY PARQUET
FLOORING OFFERS THE INTERIOR A SUBTLE
SOPHISTICATION. IT ALSO ACTS AS A HALFWAY
POINT SO THE BLACK METAL-FRAMED BEDS DO
NOT BECOME TOO DOMINANT.

less is moor

THIS PAGE NUMEROUS PATTERNED ELEMENTS CAN
BE SAVED FROM BECOMING OVERWHELMING BY THE
GROUNDING SUPPLIED BY ONE OR TWO WHITE WALLS.
HERE, ANIMAL REFERENCES AND REPEATING PATTERNS
COMBINE FOR AN INTRICATE MOORISH AMBIENCE.

culture clash

OPPOSITE CLASHING PATTERNED PATCHWORK QUILTS
ADD ENORMOUS AMOUNTS OF CHARACTER, WHILE THE
REST OF THE INTERIOR IS KEPT SIMPLE IN WHITE AND
PALE TIMBER. AN IVORY BESTLITE BL2 FROM DANISH
COMPANY GUBI OFFERS A SOFT VINTAGE QUALITY IN
TUNE WITH THE QUILTS.

Even the simplest room can be dressed up with a beautifully crafted quilt. The secret to tasteful bed covering is a restrained colour palette, with various elements restricted to a family of tones.

ABOVE LEFT OVERSIZED HEADBOARDS HAVE BEEN A TREND IN RECENT YEARS AND HERE THE CONCEPT IS EXTRAPOLATED TO BECOME AN ENTIRE WALL. THE GEOMETRIC WALLPAPER IS KEPT EXTREMELY SUBTLE SO THE PATTERN IS JUST READABLE. PILLOWS WITH A FIGURATIVE PRINT ADD INTEREST.

ABOVE VINTAGE TIMBER BEAMS ARE RELIEVED OF THEIR NORMAL BROWN TONES WITH SOME JUDICIOUS WHITEWASHING. THE RESULTING ALL-WHITE ROOM IS THEN GIVEN A DELICATE DECORATIVE TREATMENT COURTESY OF A BUTTONED HEADBOARD IN SOFT BLUE AND A MATCHING BED COVER.

LEFT THE CONCEPT OF BEDROOM AS TEMPLE REQUIRES A STRONG MINIMALIST HAND. HERE THE OWNERS HAVE OPTED FOR A BLACK STAINED FLOOR SO THE WHITE BED APPEARS TO FLOAT. COCOONED BY FLOOR-TO-CEILING WHITE DRAPES, THE ROOM HAS A ZEN-LIKE QUALITY.

modern twist

THE TIMBER DETAILS FOUND IN THE
FRENCH DOORS AND MIRROR ARE
CLEVERLY MODERNISED BY DUCK
EGG BLUE PAINTED FLOORBOARDS.
TWENTIETH CENTURY DESIGN CLASSICS
SUCH AS THE JIELDE FLOOR LIGHT AND
EAMES LCW CHAIR ADD A HINT OF
LOW-KEY ECLECTICISM.

fresh supplies

AGAINST A CRISP WHITE BACKGROUND, THESE SEVENTIES-INSPIRED
TIE-DYED CUSHIONS AND PLASTIC TABLE LAMP COMBINE AQUATIC
BLUES WITH APPLE GREEN. WITH THE ADDITION OF A LITTLE TIMBER,
THE INTERIOR TAKES ON A HEALTHY NORDIC FRESHNESS.

in tone

LEFT THE CO-ORDINATED GREY-BROWN TONES OF THE ARTWORK, PARQUET FLOOR AND LINEN BED COVERING CREATE A CALM GROUNDED ATMOSPHERE AGAINST AIRY WHITE WALLS AND CEILING. SURPRISING HITS OF BLUE ARE ADDED BY THE THROW AND TABLE LAMP.

french flair

RIGHT VINTAGE ENAMELLED PENDANT LIGHTS AND A BEDSPREAD IN SEA GREEN SET THE TONE FOR A ROOM WITH A STRONG SENSE OF THE EARLY INDUSTRIAL AGE. A BLACK AND WHITE PHOTOGRAPH, MONOGRAMMED HOTEL PILLOWCASES AND EIFFEL TOWER ORNAMENTS ALL CONTRIBUTE TO THE PARISIAN ATMOSPHERE.

bed time

AGAINST A SETTING OF ALL-WHITE DECORATIVE
ELEGANCE, A CONTEMPORARY OFF-YELLOW BED
BY TURKISH DESIGNERS AUTOBAN PROVIDES AN
INSPIRED CENTREPIECE. THE BED'S CURVED WINGS
HAVE A POETIC QUALITY THAT COMPLEMENTS THE
ELABORATE PLASTER AND TIMBER MOULDINGS.

ABOVE LEFT SOMETIMES A SIMPLE GRAPHIC OR OVERSIZED ITEM IS ALL A ROOM NEEDS. HERE, A TYPOGRAPHIC ARTWORK ABOVE THE BED STRIDENTLY STATES 'OVERRIDE'. THE WHITE WALLS, DOORS AND FLOOR PROVIDE A CALM, GALLERY-LIKE ENVIRONMENT FOR THIS BOLD ARTISTIC EXPRESSION TO RESONATE.

ABOVE NATURAL TONES ARE INTRODUCED TO THE MINIMALIST SPACE BY A BAMBOO LADDER, LARGE ARTWORK OF TRANSLUCENT LEAVES AND THE TIMBER FLOOR. STORAGE BAYS ARE KEPT HIGH SO AS NOT TO DISRUPT THE CALM.

LEFT STRONG VISUAL INTEREST IS CREATED BY SWEEPING CURVED WALLS WITH REPEATING TIMBER VERTICALS. THE FOCUS BECOMES THE SHAPE, SHADOWS AND LIGHT. A PALE TIMBER FLOOR ACTS AS A BRIDGE BETWEEN THE ULTRA-WHITE RUG AND THE TIMBER BLADES.

4

EDUARDO LONGO HOUSE, SÃO PAULO

*Casa Bola began as an audacious
experiment in high-density housing
before becoming home to Eduardo Longo
and his family in the Seventies. White,
with its rigour and expansive properties,
was the interior colour of choice for
creating this utopian space.*

'*Rounded smooth corners blur the limits of small spaces
and bring that sensuous feeling.*' **Eduardo Longo**

'WHITE IS ENLARGING AND WHITE IS...WHITE,' says architect Eduardo Longo of the sensuous interior of Casa Bola — a tribute to the concentrated power of white. While the exterior is a bright blue sphere, his interest was primarily with the resolution of the interior spaces, and the exterior 'resulted from inner divisions and openings', he says.

Longo's original vision was for an alternative solution to inner-city housing, made up of a mega-structure containing a multitude of spheres. Each sphere would be an individual apartment, and would be configured in such a way within the structure to allow the maximum of light, air flow and privacy for the residents. As a means of convincing others of the viability of his scheme, he built an 8:10 model (1974–79), covering a tubular iron skeleton in 2cm ferrocement, on his flat-roofed office in downtown São Paulo. He proceeded to live there with his wife and two children.

The house is an exercise in economy, with furniture conceptualised and formed as part of the architectural plan. To that end, pieces for every room are of concrete moulded in organic curves that make the structure and its interior fittings appear as one. Whether a kitchen bench, a bed or a tiny bathroom, reminiscent of those found on a yacht, the integration is absolute. 'Rounded smooth corners blur the limits of small spaces and bring that sensuous feeling,' says Longo.

While merely a 'coincidence of purpose', the ideas around boatbuilding ('compactness, lightness and rounded hull') were of use to Longo as he sought volume without weight. The spare, considered approach of nautical design served him well.

The interior is quite remarkable. White, whether opaque or glossy, is the uniting element of a series of levels and half levels as one moves through the space. The entrance is on the middle level along with with kitchen, dining and guest bathroom; three bedroom suites, storage and laundry areas are located below, and the naturally lit living space with views of the city, and a terrace, positioned at the top of the sphere. All are connected via a central staircase which threads through the levels.

There is a certain levity in the treatment of the spaces — a decorative hammock (white, of course) hangs in the centre of the living space, just as a cheeky bunch of bananas provides a shot of yellow in the spotless kitchen. Taking this sense of play one step further, the exit from the top of the sphere is a chute in which the brave can hurtle, big-dipper style, back down to ground level.

It is not a home for excess possessions but with children, surely maintaining the original purity of the vision was a challenge? 'It is difficult not to collect stuff but it was one of the premises of the concept — low consumerism,' says Longo.

THE BEDROOMS TAKE ON
A CABIN-LIKE QUALITY AS
EVERYTHING IS MOULDED TO THE
EXACT FUNCTIONS OF THE ROOM.
THE SOFT, ROUNDED EDGES
CREATE THE SENSUOUS QUALITY
LONGO SOUGHT IN HIS DESIGN
AND THE ADDITION OF WHITE
BEDDING MAINTAINS THE SPARE
SIMPLICITY OF THE AESTHETIC.

PERHAPS THE MOST POETIC
SPACE IN THE HOUSE, THE
LIVING ROOM IS FILLED WITH
DIFFUSED LIGHT THROUGH
THE BILLOWING OPAQUE
CURTAIN TREATMENT. THE
USE OF A FINELY CRAFTED
DECORATIVE HAMMOCK
IMBUES THE SPACE WITH
A SENSE OF ROMANCE,
CREATING A VERY COMPLETE,
IF SLIGHTLY SURREAL,
INTERIOR WORLD.

THE REFLECTED LIGHT FROM THE INTENSE BLUE OF THE EXTERIOR IS A REMINDER THAT
THERE IS A WORLD OUTSIDE THE PROTECTED WHITE COCOON. THE SIMPLE STAIRWAY,
WITH ITS SOFT PROFILE, MANAGES TO BE AT ONCE FUTURISTIC AND TIMELESS –
LIKE THE MUCH USED STEPS IN AN ANCIENT GREEK VILLAGE.

BATH- ROOMS

IF EVER THERE WAS A ROOM MADE FOR WHITE, IT'S THE BATHROOM. Whether compact or generous, it allows light to bounce off walls to create a clean, bright solution. It is also an elegant backdrop to any interior treatment — as bathrooms become larger, the decorating scope extends to take in baths in spa-like proportions, freestanding furniture and even art, alongside inventive material mixes. And, as interior designer Meryl Hare puts it: 'Using white in a bathroom is intuitive. After all, it is the room to which you retreat to clean and refresh your body (and soul).'

While clean lines and precision find natural expression in the bathroom, there are numerous ways to add personality. White tiles remain popular yet can take on different looks depending on their shape, configuration, grouting — dark or light — and application. For example, mosaic tiles shot with silver can cover every surface; brick tiles can be confined to the shower recess or form a half-tiled wall, leaving the upper section for art, decorative mirrors and shelving. As designers develop art tiles, the scope for visually interesting, yet still practical, wall treatments increases.

Bathrooms are all about the material mix. For example, when used in simple slabs, carrara marble, with its predominantly white colouration and subtle pale grey veining, imparts a cool modernity. One element, such as glass or timber, dialled up, and another down, can make all the difference. Combine this with interesting fittings — a black washbasin will give the room a masculine feel whereas an ornate gilded mirror denotes glamour.

Bathrooms need a stylistic identity. A vintage bathtub sets up the expectation of limed lining boards, an enamel light fitting and old industrial shelving. If the key piece is a chandelier or elegant upholstered chair, let the other elements pivot around that choice. Practically speaking, various forms of plastic furniture are perfect for wet areas and can provide an interesting, lightweight way to introduce colour and shape. A glazed ceramic drum stool from China or timber accessories from Japan are ways to pull in subtle cultural references. However don't try to mix styles — the space is too small to accommodate more than one at a time.

black economy

A SOPHISTICATED LOOK IS POSSIBLE BY
SIMPLY MARRYING WHITE WALLS WITH
BLACK FURNITURE COMPONENTS. HERE,
A VINTAGE CHEST OF DRAWERS IS
REPURPOSED AND USED AS THE VANITY
FOR A SURFACE-MOUNTED BASIN. THE
BLACK IS REPEATED IN OTHER ELEMENTS
SUCH AS THE RADIATOR AND ARTWORK.

ABOVE LEFT CONTRAST IS CENTRAL TO THIS INTERIOR AS A BLACK FLOOR ACCENTUATES THE WHITE CLAW-FOOT BATH, MAKING IT THE KEY FEATURE DESPITE THE INTENSITY OF THE GEOMETRIC BUSSACO TILES BY THE GRAPHIC ARTIST EMMANUEL BOSSUET.

ABOVE HIGHLY ARCHITECTURAL IN NATURE, THE BATH AND WASHBASIN ARE FASHIONED FROM STONE IN LONG, LOW VOLUMES TO FORM TWO PERPENDICULAR BALANCING BOXES. CAREFUL ATTENTION TO THE WAY TILES MEET AT THE DIFFERENT SURFACES ACHIEVES THE NECESSARY PERFECTION REQUIRED.

LEFT WHEN IN DOUBT, YOU CAN ALWAYS RELY ON A SEA OF EXPRESSIVE CARRARA MARBLE TO CREATE A LUXURIOUS BATHROOM. HERE, THE EXAGGERATED GREY VEINING FOUND IN CARRARA IS SUBDUED BY THE USE OF A SIMPLE WHITE PAINTED CEILING AND WALLS ABOVE PICTURE RAIL HEIGHT.

GLASS MOSAIC TILES FORM
A SEAMLESS OPEN SPACE OF
LINEAR PLANES PUNCTUATED
ONLY BY AN EGG-SHAPED BATH
AND SIMPLE RECESSES. THE
TILE FEATURE DESIGNED BY
ARCHITECT GREG LYNN USES
A SUBTLE FLOW OF COLOUR
THROUGH FIVE PEARLESCENT
SHADES OF WHITE AND BROWN.

height advantage

IN THIS ATTIC-STYLE BATHROOM THE BATH IS
GIVEN A HEIGHTENED LEVEL OF IMPORTANCE
BY BEING MOUNTED ON A RAISED PLINTH –
PART OF A NUMBER OF TILED MODULES THAT
CREATE AN INTERESTING LANDSCAPE.

in proportion
A LONG LOW TROUGH-LIKE
BASIN IN PALE STONE IS
CLEVERLY CONTRASTED
BY A VERTICAL LADDER.
THIS BLACKENED TOWEL
RAIL LADDER LINKS
PROPORTIONALLY AND
TONALLY TO THE SHELF
BELOW THE BASIN AND
THE LARGE BLACK-
FRAMED WINDOWS.

THIS PAGE, LEFT SMALL BATHROOMS CAN OFTEN BE AIRLESS AND DARK, BUT HERE THE OWNERS HAVE OPTED FOR THE OPENNESS OF A FINE STEEL-FRAMED GLASS DOOR.

THIS PAGE, RIGHT THIS LIGHT-FILLED BATHROOM IN A CONVERTED SPANISH WAREHOUSE HAS A TOUCH OF TWENTIES GLAMOUR ADDED THROUGH THE USE OF CUT GLASS MIRRORS, PERIOD TAPWARE AND GENEROUS, SOFTLY ROUNDED BASIN AND BATH FORMS.

OPPOSITE PAGE, LEFT THE SPARTAN MINIMALISM OF THIS BATHROOM FEATURES AN INTERESTING COMBINATION OF LUXURY AND INDUSTRIAL MATERIALS – CARRARA MARBLE WITH A CEILING IN ROUGH-FORMED CONCRETE.

OPPOSITE PAGE, RIGHT CREATIVELY UTILISING OLD-FASHIONED STYLES IN A NEW RUSTIC WAY, THIS BATHROOM BRINGS TOGETHER SURFACE-MOUNTED SHOWER FITTINGS, A PARTIALLY STRIPPED CAST IRON BATH AND PLANTATION SHUTTERS.

The use of traditional materials and fittings in contemporary
interiors can add a special quality that brings further sophistication
to clean-cut modern architecture. Using a combination of white,
grey, black and silver offers a huge range of creative possibilities.

beyond a shadow of grout

SMALL WHITE TILES CAN BE GIVEN A FAR MORE POWERFUL
APPEARANCE SIMPLY BY GROUTING IN A CONTRASTING COLOUR.
CONCRETE GREY GROUT AMPLIFIES THEIR REPETITIOUS
GEOMETRIC NATURE AND ENHANCES THE SEVENTIES FEEL.

ABOVE SOPHISTICATION HAS BEEN EXPRESSED IN THIS BATHROOM THROUGH THE USE OF A PAIR OF CLASSICALLY INSPIRED WALL LAMPS AND A CURVACEOUS MIRROR. PALE MOSAIC-TILED WALLS AND WHITE MARBLE COMBINE WITH LIGHT TIMBER TO CREATE A RESTRAINED BEAUTY.

ABOVE RIGHT THE HORIZONTAL EMPHASIS OF A BANK OF IDENTICAL HOPPER WINDOWS IS REINFORCED BY A MARBLE BENCHTOP WITH REPEATING DRAINING LINES ALONG ITS SURFACE. THESE LINES DRAW THE EYE TO THE WINDOWS AND THE VIEW BEYOND.

RIGHT THIS BATHROOM FEATURES THE SAME SQUARE WHITE TILES ON THE FLOOR AS THE WALLS. THE STAINLESS STEEL DOUBLE WASHBASIN USES WALL-MOUNTED LEVER TAPS AND GIVES THE BATHROOM A SENSE OF CLEANLINESS AND ORDER.

at the outside

THIS PAGE LUSCIOUS GREENERY COMBINES WITH AN INTEGRATED CONCRETE BATH AND A DIAPHANOUS CEILING OF FINE SLATTED TIMBER. SURPRISING HITS OF COLOUR CONTEMPORISE IT.

true colours

OPPOSITE THE OWNER HAS EMBRACED THE ARTWORK AND CHOSEN RESIN WASHBASINS IN AN OLD-FASHIONED RED AND SOMBRE BLACK. CONTRASTING BRASS AND CHROME PLATE IS APPLIED TO THE TAPWARE ON THE DUAL BASINS.

Strong colour can, if used carefully, enhance otherwise monochromatic modern interiors. Colour of this type tends to pop from the background and take over. Keeping the items relatively small and contained prevents overkill.

take shape

OPPOSITE THE POETIC SHAPE OF THE WINDOW ALCOVE IS ECHOED BY THE OVAL BATH. THE STONE COLOUR CHOSEN TO SURROUND IT IS A PERFECT TONAL MATCH FOR THE AGED TIMBER BEAMS (JUST SEEN).

room service

THIS PAGE THIS BATHROOM EXUDES A SENSE OF THE COLONIAL ERA WITH AN OVERHEAD FAN AND FREESTANDING BATH COMPLETE WITH EXPOSED TAP FITTINGS. THE HIGHLY POLISHED FLOOR TILES CLEVERLY MIRROR THE COLOUR OF THE CEILING.

ABOVE THE FORTIES LOOK OF WHITE GLAZED BRICKS IS NICELY REPRODUCED HERE WITH IMMACULATELY LAID TILES COMPLETED BY AN ORIGINAL MARBLEISED GREEN WASHBASIN, CHROMED WALL LIGHTS AND MIRROR IN A DECO STYLE. THE GLAZED PANEL TIMBER DOOR LIGHTENS THE LOOK.

ABOVE RIGHT WITH SMOOTH CURVES, THIS BATHROOM HAS THE APPEARANCE OF THOSE FOUND IN LUXURY YACHTS. THE THE ALL-WHITE POLISHED CONCRETE INTERIOR IS GIVEN A LIFT BY THE COLOURFUL CUPBOARD DOOR BENEATH THE FORMED WASHBASIN, AND THE DOOR FOLLOWS THE SHAPELY AESTHETIC.

RIGHT THE USE OF SQUARE AND RECTANGULAR TILES IN THE SAME COLOUR AND FINISH PROVIDES A SEEMINGLY RANDOM GEOMETRIC LOOK TO THE BATHROOM WALLS. THE DE STIJL-STYLE PATTERN CONTINUES WITH A CLEVER TIMBER SHELF DETAIL THAT FLOWS ASYMMETRICALLY FROM THE DOORFRAME.

by contrast

AN ELABORATE LEAF AND RIBBON
GARLAND IN WHITE PAINTED PLASTER
PROVIDES A LYRICAL NOTE. OPULENT
BRONZE BATH FEET ARE BALANCED
BY SIMPLE OAK PARQUETRY.

dormer view

THE DRAMATIC SIZE AND SHAPE OF THE DORMER
WINDOW ARE ARCHITECTURALLY SIGNIFICANT
BUT THE SIMPLE WHITEWASHED FLOORBOARDS,
TRADITIONAL BATH AND WASHBASIN BRING THE
BATHROOM BACK TO A MORE HUMAN LEVEL.

FADED GRANDEUR IS CLEVERLY SUBVERTED BY THE USE OF WHITE BLOCKS THAT LEAD
TO A SMALL HIGH BATH. THIS CONTEMPORARY DEVICE IS BEAUTIFULLY EXECUTED WITHIN
THE TROMPE L'OEIL-PAINTED INTERIOR.

light touch

THE EXTENSIVE USE OF WHITE
TILES FORMS A RESTRAINED
BACKDROP TO THIS OTHERWISE
HIGHLY DECORATIVE BATHROOM.
COMPLETE WITH CUT GLASS
CHANDELIER AND YELLOW
BUTTON-BACKED SLIPPER CHAIR, IT
USES GLASS PANELS IN THE CEILING
TO BRING IN AN ABUNDANCE OF
NATURAL LIGHT AND INCREASE
ITS PERCEIVED SIZE.

ABOVE LEFT COVERED FLOOR TO CEILING IN WHITE TILES IN SEVERAL DIFFERENT SIZES AND PATTERNS, THIS BATHROOM SHOWS HOW SUBTLE DECORATION CAN BE INCORPORATED INTO AN ALL-WHITE SCHEME. THE SHOWER AREA IS BELOW A LIGHT WELL TO PROVIDE PLENTY OF SUNLIGHT.

ABOVE THIS AIRY BATHROOM USES WHITE TILES AND LOW WALLS TO FRAME THE GARDEN OUTLOOK. COLOUR AND COMPLEXITY IS ADDED IN THE FORM OF A BEAUTIFUL GEOMETRIC TILED FLOOR WITH THE OCHRE YELLOW COLOUR CONTINUED IN THE SHAKER-STYLE CABINET THAT HOUSES THE WASHBASIN.

LEFT BANKS OF GLASS LOUVRES ON TWO WALLS BRING LIGHT AND VENTILATION INTO THIS GENEROUS BATHROOM. THE VIRTUAL REMOVAL OF ALL FITTINGS THROUGH A PARTIALLY SUNKEN BATH AND A CEILING SHOWER KEEP THE SPACE AS OPEN, SIMPLE AND UNADORNED AS POSSIBLE.

in shape

THIS ENSUITE BATHROOM USES THE CONTRAST OF A FREESTANDING EGG-SHAPED BATH AGAINST THE REPEATED GEOMETRY OF BRICK-STYLE TILES. THE GOLDEN DIAMOND PENDANT LIGHT CREATES A THIRD SHAPE. A DOSE OF ORGANIC WARMTH IS PROVIDED BY A WALL OF ORIENTED STRAND BOARD (OSB).

pattern play

LEFT A FEATURE WALL OF GEOMETRIC BISAZZA GLASS MOSAIC TILES IN THE TREILLAGE DESIGN BY PATRICIA URQUIOLA ARE REFLECTED BY A LARGE WALL MIRROR. CLASSIC CARRARA MARBLE IS USED ON THE FLOOR TO PREVENT THE WHOLE SCHEME FROM BECOMING TOO OVERWHELMING.

green gauge

RIGHT REVEALING A CONTAINED ELEMENT OF COLOUR WITHIN THE CONTEXT OF AN OTHERWISE ALL-WHITE ROOM CAN BE A LOVELY SURPRISE. HERE, THE GREY-GREEN COLOUR OF A TERRAZZO SHOWER RECESS IS ENHANCED BY THE GREEN TINT OF THE GLASS DOOR.

5

SUSAN FRASER HOUSE, LHERM

The charms of an 18th century French maison de maître proved irresistible to a writer who embraced the monumental task of sensitive refurbishment. White paint on all surfaces, including underfoot and overhead, was the final uplifting touch.

THE RE-IMAGINING OF SPACE REQUIRES A PARTICULAR SKILL, but the execution often entails serious stamina in order to balance retaining that vision and pushing through the harsh realities. Such was the experience of Australian writer Susan Fraser. It is a shame it was not recorded by a restoration TV show as it had all the hallmarks of good television. The house was bought in the blink of an eye after coming across the picturesque village of Lherm in southwestern France. 'We turned down a side path next to the church and there it was — this beautiful *maison de maître* for sale,' says Fraser.

The romance of the place was not lost on her: a simple, freestanding house (like a child's drawing, she says) in the local Quercy stone with its light-catching, honey-pink colouration. The purple hydrangeas bordering the front terrace, and the placement of the house in an unspoilt medieval village opposite a grassy square and a beautiful 12th century church sold it in a moment.

Inside was a different story but, coming from a family of architects (her father, Viv, and sister Sharon are in the profession), she had a sense of how the house could evolve. 'We measured everything up and took photos for my father, and after many phone conversations with him back in Australia, he sent us the plans to convert,' says Fraser.

The design intent was to retain the character of the 18th century four-level house but open it up and make connections between areas that had no relationship on the original plan. For example, the earth-floored basement, which had been used for animals and storage, became a kitchen/bathroom/storage area and was linked to the living space via a staircase. This first level living space had been a series of poky rooms, the walls of which were demolished. 'We were armed with hammers, stupid grins and not much sense,' says Fraser. The grins turned to tears as summer gave way to a chill autumn and a freezing winter. Bitter winds whistled through the house, the roof leaked, there was barely any heating and only one oddly positioned toilet in the sitting room.

But gradually joy resurfaced as the house came together, with white playing a pivotal role in the rejuvenation process. Normally a stickler for the retention of natural materials, Fraser found that some of the timbers were too decayed to remedy and some exposed beams too haphazardly sized because they were never intended to be seen. She felt they also created a heavy, somewhat depressing feel, but as soon as they were painted white, the ceiling was transformed and 'lifted'.

The floorboards in the living/dining rooms are a 'pure' white satin floorpaint, whereas the walls in the living room, bedrooms and upstairs bathroom are white satin but with a very, very subtle 'rose' hue. 'In the afternoon sunlight the colour is magnificent...like a reflection of the rose hue in the Quercy stone,' says Fraser.

MUCH OF THE FOCUS OF THE RENOVATION WAS IN THE REMOVAL OF
FALSE CEILINGS AND INTERNAL PARTITIONS, WHICH HAD BEEN BUILT
OVER THE PAST 100 YEARS, TO REVEAL THE ORIGINAL STONE, TIMBER
FLOORS, HANDCUT FLOOR JOISTS AND CEILING BEAMS.

*'A "retired" master builder helped us convert the basement
– he taught us how to point the stone and lay the tinted
concrete floor. He was brilliant.' Susan Fraser*

BEAUTIFUL OLD ARMCHAIRS,
WITH GREAT SHAPES BUT DAMAGED
COVERS, HAVE BEEN DRAPED WITH
WHITE FABRIC AND THROWS TO
ENHANCE THE SIMPLICITY OF THE
SUNLIT ROOMS. 'SOFT WHITES AND
CREAMS JUST WORK,' SAYS FRASER.

'THE LIGHT IN THE SPACE IS MAGICAL – PARTICULARLY IN THE LIVING/DINING AREA AND THE BEDROOMS,' SAYS FRASER. CAREFULLY SOURCED PIECES OF FURNITURE FILL THE HOUSE, AND THE BATHROOM (OPPOSITE) HAS BEEN RESTORED TO BE IN KEEPING WITH THE ORIGINAL BUILDING. 'WE SEARCHED FOR AN OLD SABOT BATHTUB TO ENSURE THE BATHROOM FELT AS IF IT HAD ALWAYS BEEN THERE,' SHE SAYS.

STAIRS & HALLS

WE TEND TO THINK OF STAIRS AND HALLWAYS AS ANIMATED SPACES WE MOVE THROUGH, often quickly, to get from one place to the next. Despite their practical purpose, they are frequently elevated to a position of architectural power within buildings – creating bold, graphic transitions of level, directing the eye to a visual destination. White often helps express the form of a staircase and lighten a hallway or landing in a way that is both functional and inspiring. Hence, rather than thinking of them as robbing a home of valuable floor space, it's better to regard them as essential to a building's flow, sense of space and an integral component in the overall aesthetic.

Stairs are, by definition, dynamic. Whether a sharp diagonal, a spiral or fashioned in a sweeping arc, they all add drama and character regardless of their scale and material. Their sculptural qualities make them well-suited to interesting interior juxtapositions: a spare modernist curve of white in a 19th century building, a graphic zigzag paired with an ornate balustrade or a flash of unexpected colour in a white tread. Every small stylistic choice will take on greater significance due to the rhythmic, repetitive nature of the stair's construction. There is a rich opportunity for decorative application within the context of white, be it the mixing of materials, the addition of carpet or the tiling of the adjacent walls. In the context of stairways, there is something luxurious about a landing. A place not to move through but to stop and contemplate the world — a window and chair are the only essentials.

Halls are less about shape and more about placement and size. When adjacent to, or leading to, a courtyard or garden, an additional element immediately becomes part of the scheme. Where this isn't possible, they benefit from being generous in size with some form of natural light, from skylights or windows along their length. Hallways not only link spaces physically but also visually, permitting glimpses of rooms at either end or off to the side. The layering of rooms is a common architectural trick to create a sense of anticipation of what lies ahead. Not everything needs to be revealed at once.

sculptural form

WHILE A FUNCTIONAL NECESSITY, STAIRS CAN BE AN EXPRESSIVE ELEMENT IN A HOUSE. HERE THE SCULPTURAL SHAPE BECOMES THE HERO OF THE ROOM – ITS SMOOTH WHITE FORM CONTRASTING WITH THE TEXTURAL QUALITIES OF THE FORMED CONCRETE WALLS.

great heights

THE HEIGHT OF THE ENTRY HALL IS
EMPHASISED BY A HUGE WALL CLOCK.
THE LARGE EXPANSE OF WHITE WALLS
IS OFFSET BY DUCK-EGG BLUE AND
RUSTIC RED IN THE FRONT DOOR
AND BRICK STAIR TREADS.

ABOVE THIS LIGHT-FILLED HALLWAY PASSES THROUGH MULTIPLE ZONES, ALLOWING FOR DISTANT GLIMPSES INTO OTHER ROOMS. THIS HEIGHTENS THE INTRIGUE IN AN INTERIOR AND CREATES SPATIAL DEPTH. IN THIS PARTICULAR EXAMPLE THE ZONES ARE OPENED OR CLOSED WITH LARGE SLIDING DOORS THAT KEEP AREAS INTIMATE OR ALLOW THEM TO FLOW INTO EACH OTHER.

ABOVE RIGHT THE STRUCTURE OF A STAIRCASE CAN ADD A LARGE DOSE OF ARCHITECTURAL INTEREST TO A ROOM. HERE, THE STAIRCASE USES UNUSUAL TIMBER DETAILING TO PROVIDE A GRAPHIC ZIGZAG SHAPE THAT OFFSETS THE ROUNDED BENT STEEL FURNITURE. THE PAULISTANO ARMCHAIRS AND KAEKO COFFEE TABLE ARE BOTH FROM FRENCH BRAND OBJEKTO.

RIGHT THE MEETING POINT OF THESE POLISHED CONCRETE STAIRS AND WHITE WALL-MOUNTED SHELVING UNIT CREATES A STRONG MOTIF THAT IS IN STRIKING CONTRAST TO THE FREEFORM WALL BEHIND IT. HINTS OF RIGID GEOMETRY ARE INTEGRATED WITH AN ABUNDANCE OF ORGANIC CURVES.

Stair voids offer the opportunity to incorporate some seriously overscale lighting. The increased headroom works particularly well for long clusters of lights or sculptural fittings.

light well

OPPOSITE THE LARGE-SCALE LIGHT IS PERFECT
FOR A STAIR VOID. MADE FROM MULTIPLE RICE
PAPER LANTERNS THAT PROVIDE A SLIGHTLY
TEXTURAL WHITE TO BALANCE THE PAINTWORK,
THE FITTING ALSO CREATES LOVELY SHADOWS.

attic order

THIS PAGE MAKING FULL USE OF THE FORMER
WAREHOUSE'S PITCHED ROOF, THE BEDROOM
IS CAREFULLY SLOTTED IN AT ONE END WHILE
A WIDE WALKWAY JOINS THE TWO ENDS OF THE
ATTIC. THE LIMED FLOORING AND WHITE PAINTED
WOODWORK KEEP IT FEELING AIRY AND OPEN.

THIS PAGE, LEFT THE BLACK ZIGZAG OF THE STAIR TREAD CREATES A GRAPHIC BREAK BETWEEN THE OLD-WORLD HANDRAIL AND THE MORE CONTEMPORARY WALL-MOUNTED CABINET.

THIS PAGE, RIGHT SUSPENDED TREADS APPEAR TO DEFY GRAVITY AND ALLOW AREAS TO REMAIN OPEN WHILE ADDING A BOLD SHAPE. IN THIS MONOCHROME KITCHEN SPACE, THE WHITE TIMBER STAIRS ALSO CONSTITUTE A STRONG SCULPTURAL FORM.

OPPOSITE PAGE, LEFT THIS GRAND STAIRCASE FEATURES THE TRADITIONAL OPULENCE OF A PLUSH CARPETED STAIR RUNNER AND A STONE-CAPPED LANDING AREA AT ITS BASE.

OPPOSITE PAGE, RIGHT WITH SOMETHING OF THE LOOK OF A DONALD JUDD ARTWORK, THESE STEEP WHITE STAIRS FLOAT MAGICALLY UP THE WALL WITHOUT EXTRANEOUS HANDRAILS. THE GLOWING WHITENESS IS ALMOST ETHEREAL.

Stairs bring a much-needed change to the vertical and horizontal norms of architecture. Whether they are spiral, diagonal or a sweeping curve, they are a thing of real beauty.

installation artwork

OPPOSITE A HALLWAY NEEDN'T BE JUST A PRACTICAL THOROUGHFARE. THIS HIGHLY PERSONAL SPACE REVEALS GLIMPSES OF AN INTERIOR WITH ESCHER-LIKE STAIRS, BLOCKS AND VOIDS. THE FACETED TIMBER WALL BALANCES THE COMPLEXITY OF THE REST OF THE INTERIOR.

height variation

THIS PAGE A COLLECTION OF MONOCHROME VERTICAL SHAPES HIGHLIGHTS THE HEIGHT OF THIS ENTRANCE HALL – FLOOR-TO-CEILING DRAPES, A WHITE PEACOCK PERCHED HIGH ON THE WALL AND A FRAMED MIRROR POSITIONED UNUSUALLY LOW.

ABOVE IN STARK CONTRAST TO THE USUAL USE OF MASSED STONE OR CONCRETE IN OUTDOOR STAIRS, THESE DELICATELY FOLDED STEEL STAIRS HAVE JUST A MINIMAL DIAGONAL SUPPORT. INTRICATE PATTERNS ARE FORMED BY THE THE SHADOWS CREATED BY THE STAIRCASE AND HANDRAIL.

ABOVE RIGHT HALLWAYS THAT FLOW AROUND AN INNER COURTYARD OR ARE ADJACENT TO AN EXTERIOR WALL ARE NOT ONLY FILLED WITH LIGHT BUT THE FRAMING GENERALLY CREATES A FASCINATING SHADOW PLAY DURING THE DAY. HERE, THE REPEATING SQUARE FRAMES ON THE RIGHT CREATE AN EVER-MOVING PATTERN ON THE FLOOR.

RIGHT THE INHERENT POWER OF THE HALLWAY IS IN ITS PROMISE OF SOMETHING BEYOND THE CURRENT ROOM. IN THIS PARTICULAR SPACE, THE COMPLEX BEAMS AND CARDBOARD SCREEN SEEM TO LEAD THE EYE TO THE BRIGHTER HALLWAY AND A MYSTERIOUS PALE BLUE DOOR IN THE DISTANCE.

fine down

STAIRS ARE RARELY AS SKELETAL
AS THIS. WITH AN IMPOSSIBLY FINE
HANDRAIL AND TIMBER TREADS
PERCHED ON STEEL BLADES, THIS
STAIRCASE SWEEPS LIGHTLY FROM THE
UPSTAIRS LIBRARY TO THE SOLIDITY OF
RANDOM FLAGSTONES BELOW.

easy elegance

THIS PAGE THIS ELEGANT MONOCHROME
ENTRANCE HALL USES CRISP WHITE WALLS
AND DARK STAINED TIMBER FLOORS FOR
A CLASSIC LOOK, BUT ADDS THE DELICATE
SOFT COLOURS OF PINK AND BEIGE AND AN
EXQUISITE VINTAGE ROBSJOHN-GIBBINGS
KLISMOS CHAIR FOR ADDED DEPTH.

below stairs

OPPOSITE THE NATURAL SYNERGY BETWEEN
LIMED TIMBER AND WHITE PLASTER IS SHOWN
TO FULL EFFECT IN THIS LONDON BASEMENT
KITCHEN AND LIVING AREA. IT BENEFITS FROM
THE LIGHT-COLOURED MATERIALS AND THE
EXTRA SCULPTURAL ELEMENT THE SHADOW
LINE BETWEEN THE STAIR AND WALL PROVIDES.

Whether in modern or traditional environments, the pattern formed by stair treads adds instant visual excitement and can easily be used as the starting point for material or stylistic choices.

ABOVE LEFT FORMED CONCRETE STAIRS DISPLACED FROM ONE SIDE TO THE OTHER CREATE AN INTERESTING VISUAL CONTRADICTION WHEN COMBINED WITH TIMBER SLATS AND STACKED STONES. AS A RESULT, THIS OUTDOOR STAIR FEELS LOOSE AND ARTISTIC, WITH A SLIGHTLY JAPANESE FEEL.

ABOVE WORKING WITHIN A SEMI-INDUSTRIAL FRAMEWORK, THIS STAIR IS LINKED TO THE STEEL-FRAME DOOR BY WAY OF BOTH MATERIAL AND PROPORTION. COLOUR IS ALSO USED TO FURTHER THE CONNECTION OF THE STAIR TO ITS SURROUNDINGS, AS SEEN IN THE DARK BLUE CARPET AND ARTWORK.

LEFT THE STAIRCASE IN THIS LONG ISLAND HOUSE SHOWS A DELIGHTFUL MIX OF SIMPLICITY AND REPETITION TO ACCENTUATE THE SCALE OF THE INTERIOR. THE HALLWAYS ARE WIDE AND OPEN – MORE LIKE ROOMS THAN THOROUGHFARES, WITH WHITE KEEPING THE VAST SPACE UNIFIED.

interior motifs

EXTREME PATTERN HAS TRANSFORMED THE STAIRCASE
AND DOOR INTO A GRAPHIC FEATURE. ALL VERTICAL
SURFACES ARE STENCILLED WITH MOROCCAN-INSPIRED
DESIGNS BY MELANIE ROYALS, WHILE ALL HORIZONTALS
REMAIN MINIMAL IN CONCRETE OR TIMBER.

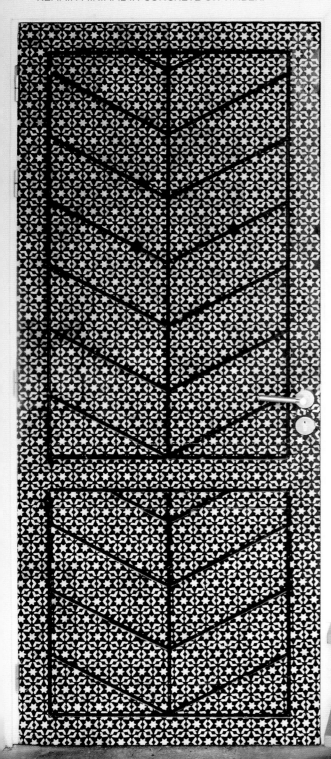

outside edge
TAKING THE STYLE OF STAIRCASE
NORMALLY FOUND IN HIGH-END
ARCHITECTURAL INTERIORS
AND PLACING IT OUTSIDE, THE
DESIGNER OF THIS RIBBON-LIKE
STEEL AND CONCRETE PIECE
HAS CREATED AN EXCITING
JUXTAPOSITION BETWEEN THE
MAN-MADE AND THE NATURAL.

vanishing point

LEFT WITH ITS OVERT MOORISH QUALITY
REINFORCED BY TERRACOTTA TILES AND METAL
STAR LAMPS, THIS BEAUTIFULLY BRIGHT HALLWAY
USES REPETITION AND SYMMETRY TO HIGHLIGHT
ITS LENGTH. A DISTANT DOOR BECOMES THE FOCAL
POINT BUT NATURAL LIGHT POURING IN FROM ONE
SIDE ADDS IMMENSE DEPTH.

halls of learning

RIGHT A HALLWAY CAN BE MANY THINGS. HERE THIS
CONVENTIONAL ENTRANCE HALL BECOMES PURE
ART PIECE WITH COLOURFUL PILLARS OF BOOKS
LEADING TO AN ECLECTIC LOUNGE ROOM BEYOND.
THE 'GATEWAY' IS GUARDED BY THE APTLY NAMED
BOLD CHAIR BY BIG GAME FOR MOUSTACHE.

CHRIS DYSON HOUSE, LONDON

It is hard to imagine this refined interior was once a fire-damaged leather garment factory. Located in Princelet Street, Spitalfields, the Georgian terrace is testament to the skill of architect Chris Dyson and his abilities to coax beauty from the unloved and neglected.

'We avoid using pure white, and usually choose a soft distempered-
looking shade of white, with grey, as this is often very flattering
both to the furniture and artworks. The modulation of light is
an important aspect of Georgian houses.' *Chris Dyson*

CHRIS DYSON, AN ARCHITECT WHO LIVES AND WORKS IN LONDON'S SPITALFIELDS, is very much a man of his context. He has renovated many houses in the area, both for himself and for clients, and understands the very essence of these distinguished old buildings. The house in Princelet Street was bought as something of a wreck, having been fire-damaged, botched back together and used as a leather garment factory for many years. Neglect had defined its recent history. Chris Dyson and his wife Sarah managed elementary repairs to make the place liveable but were eventually drawn to another property across the road at number 11. Dyson turned this into a gallery and architectural office space with family living areas above it. After some years, and an inheritance to fund the plans, he turned his attention back to the original property and used his accumulated knowledge to revitalise the house. Externally, he brought it visually in line with its neighbours, partly by replacing windows and replacing an ugly grey façade with reclaimed bricks.

Internally it was a space bereft of its original fireplaces, mouldings and panelling, and so provided plenty of scope for Dyson's ability to source, commission and re-create. He is an avid collector, as can be seen in the layered nature of the house's interior decoration and, with the rich hunting ground of Spitalfields markets a stone's throw away, he is never short of a new and fascinating artefact.

The beauty of the house partly lies in the soft colour of the oak boards and the paint choices from Farrow & Ball (Great White, All White and Shaded White). Combined with a dove grey, the subtle range of whites gently emphasises features such as the fireplace and the arched alcoves that flank it. However, says Dyson, 'I try to avoid making features of architectural details as this can make an interior look very fussy.'

While the word eclectic may be overused, it sometimes fits, as in the case of Dyson's home. His unerring eye finds ways that disparate objects, artworks and furniture pieces, from different eras, cultures and materials, can happily co-exist. For example, a row of sheep skulls lines a windowsill, smart Matthew Hilton armchairs sit either side of the fireplace and an IKEA four-poster graces the master bedroom. It is a mix-and-match philosophy of the best sort.

The kitchen and dining room are located in the basement and hence in need of light, so while the white is sharper and cleaner, the mix of old and new continues. Blue and white Delft crockery (inherited from Sarah's father) is displayed in white-painted, custom-built shelves while dining chairs by Matthew Hilton surround a table designed by Dyson. The dynamic is always present — confirming the past and the history of the house but refusing to be a hostage to it. The result is a home with the best of several worlds — the original Georgian proportions, the adjusted floor plan to accommodate modern life, *objets trouvés* and inherited pieces that make a space feel interesting and loved, bespoke elements that are new and those that are carefully re-created. And the most skilful element of all is that it feels completely effortless and utterly genuine.

INHERITED PIECES, SUCH AS THE CHAIR AND DELFT CROCKERY, ARE DISPLAYED IN FRONT OF PANELLING AND SHELVING DESIGNED BY DYSON. WIDE DOORWAYS CREATE A FLOW OF SPACE, GETTING LIGHTER AND STRONGER AS YOU MOVE THROUGH THE HOUSE. FURNITURE PIECES MIX MODERN DESIGNER WORKS WITH VINTAGE FINDS.

THE BATHROOM EXPLOITS THE FUNCTIONAL SIMPLICITY OF WHITE BUTCHER'S TILES
ALONGSIDE CLASSIC BATHROOM FITTINGS, WHILE THE BEDROOM'S DECORATION ILLUSTRATES
THE EFFECTIVENESS OF SPARE STYLING. A MODERN LINEAR FOUR-POSTER FROM IKEA COMBINES
WITH IMPACTFUL CARVED FURNITURE FROM QUITE ANOTHER ERA.

OUTDOOR SPACES

THE USE OF WHITE OUTSIDE — BE IT A PAINTED VERANDAH OR EXPANSIVE WALL TREATMENT — has a simplicity and formality which works well as a context to express the shape of furniture pieces and garden sculptures, not to mention an entire building. With historic precedents in the clustered buildings of the Greek islands or rigid formality of the Bauhaus in northern Europe, it's plain to see that white exteriors can take very different stylistic directions. Just as when used indoors, white acts as an anchor, bringing visual cohesiveness to what is placed in front of it.

White is also a great natural foil to the variegated shades of green in foliage and becomes a perfect surface for the play of shadow and movement. Because white is such a complex tone, with thousands of variations, it is possible to find just the right version of white for each context. A soft white marries with common outdoor materials such as timber, concrete and stone that come in a tonal range from pale brown to grey or black. This combination of materials, with their inherent texture and grain, adds a great deal of depth to an exterior and contrasts effectively with the precision of white.

When white is used in large expanses, such as on rendered walls, the effect is to bounce light around the space — a perfect choice for covered areas and internal courtyards. There is also the classic appeal of the white-painted verandah, in which the floorboards are also painted to create that sense of a covered outdoor room. Simple furniture pieces then become the hero of the decorating story.

While white is a strong backdrop, it is also an effective choice for furniture pieces, as shades of white work well in an outdoor setting. When placed with confidence, they take on a significant presence. Whether a Verner Panton S chair, a simple deckchair, modular seating or the classic Adirondack chair, they all look good against nature, near water or even in the context of white on white. With nature's palette of blue sky, water and greenery, along with white man-made objects, it's hard to go wrong.

in the shade

COVERED OUTDOOR ROOMS PROVIDE MUCH-NEEDED SHADE IN SUNNY CLIMATES. HERE, AN ALUMINIUM AND POLYETHYLENE DINING TABLE AND POLYPROPYLENE BELLINI CHAIRS ARE SET AGAINST A DARK TIMBER SLATTED WALL. THESE FURNITURE PIECES ARE VIRTUALLY INDESTRUCTIBLE, COMBINING DURABILITY AND STYLE.

holding court

DECORATIVE ARCHITECTURAL FEATURES ARE PAINTED IN SHADES OF OFF-WHITE AND TAUPE BUT A STARK WHITE TABLE CREATES A STRONG FOCAL POINT. THE MODERN LOOK OF THE S CHAIRS BY VERNER PANTON STRIKE A CHARMING CONTRAST.

ABOVE WITHIN A PRECISE WHITE STRUCTURE, THIS SPACE IS AN ECLECTIC MIX OF ERAS AND MATERIALS WITH A STRONG EMPHASIS ON THE NATURAL AND TEXTURAL – BRICKS ON THE FLOOR, A WIDE PLANKED TIMBER TABLE AND WOVEN PENDANT LAMP. POT PLANTS BRING A SENSE OF GARDEN TO THE COURTYARD.

ABOVE RIGHT REINFORCING THE TRADITIONAL LOOK OF THIS FORMER HUNTING LODGE IN UPSTATE NEW YORK, THE PAINT SCHEME USES WHITE FOR THE TIMBER CLADDING AND POSTS WITH DARK SHUTTERS AND A MATCHING TRIO OF ROCKING CHAIRS. A PALE GREY PAINTED TIMBER CEILING ADDS A SUBTLE SHIFT TO THE ALL-WHITE SCHEME.

RIGHT WITH MEMPHIS-STYLE GLASS MOSAICS IN COLOURS OF PASTEL PINK, YELLOW AND BLUE, THIS BRAZILIAN HOUSE USES A MATCHING ORGANIC SHAPE ON THE CONCRETE TERRACE AND THE OVERHANG ABOVE. THE LANGUID-LOOKING CHAISE IS MADE OF FORMED WHITE-TONED CONCRETE.

Creating areas of sun and shade around a pool is vital for maximising its use. Deep building overhangs provide cool areas for lounging while nearby plants soften the atmosphere.

soft option

OPPOSITE PLANTING RIGHT UP TO THE EDGE OF A POOL REMOVES ITS HARD-EDGED GEOMETRY AND RE-CREATES THE FEELING OF BATHING IN A RIVER OR BROOK.

hit the roof

THIS PAGE UTILISING THE ROOF TERRACE IN FLAT TERRAIN CHANGES THE VIEW'S PERSPECTIVE. HERE, BUILT-IN SEATING WITH WHITE CUSHIONS CONTRASTS WITH RENDERED CEMENT WALLS AND RUSTIC WOVEN OTTOMANS AND RUGS.

THIS PAGE, LEFT PERFORATED MESH SCREENS OFFER A DIFFUSED ELEMENT TO A HIGHLY LAYERED GRID PATTERN OF SQUARES AND RECTANGLES. THE MESH PROVIDES PRIVACY AND ADDS COMPLEXITY.

THIS PAGE, RIGHT EXTREME VERTICALITY IS ACCENTUATED WITH THE SLATTED SCREENS EMPHASISING THE HEIGHT OF THE ROOMS AND CREATING INTERESTING SHADOW PATTERNS. CLASSIC RICHARD SCHULTZ 1966 CHAIRS FOR KNOLL IN PAINTED ALUMINIUM AND MESH ARE THE PERFECT MATCH.

OPPOSITE PAGE, LEFT A SUSPENDED TABLE AND BENCH OFFER A ZEN-LIKE SPACE FOR CONTEMPLATION OF THE GREENERY BEYOND. THE SMALL SPACE IS MADE CONSIDERABLY LARGER BY ITS OUTLOOK.

OPPOSITE PAGE, RIGHT A VERTICAL GARDEN CREATES A LAYERED EFFECT WITH THE IVY-CLAD BRICK WALL OF THE HOUSE BEYOND. THE CONTINUOUS FLOW OF GREEN SOFTENS THE SMALL SPACE.

While the use of walls is effective in creating intimate spaces, making those same vertical elements into living walls adds another layer to the scheme. The inclusion of even the smallest amount of greenery is highly worthwhile.

art works

THIS PAGE A GIANT STEEL SCULPTURE BY BETTY GOLD STAMPS THE PRESENCE OF MAN IN THIS OTHERWISE NATURALLY BUSHY SETTING IN LOS ANGELES. THE FORMED CONCRETE WALL AND POOL BELOW FIT WELL WITH THE GREY-GREEN NATIVE FOLIAGE.

nature's palette

OPPOSITE SURROUNDED BY LUSH GREENERY, THIS GARDEN TERRACE IN ANTIBES IS ATTACHED TO AN ALL-WHITE, STRICTLY GEOMETRIC HOUSE. THE CONNECTION FROM HOUSE TO OUTDOORS IS ENHANCED BY THE USE OF WHITE OUTDOOR UPHOLSTERY AND WHITE SIDE TABLES. THE BLUE OUTDOOR CHAIRS ARE FRAME FROM PAOLA LENTI.

ABOVE THE WHITE GEOMETRIC ENVELOPE – THE OVERRIDING FEATURE OF THIS HOUSE IN LOS ANGELES – IS GIVEN A NATURAL TACTILE ELEMENT WITH SLATTED TIMBER SCREENS. THIS, AND AN ORGANICALLY SHAPED HARDOY BUTTERFLY CHAIR, CONTRASTS WITH THE RIGID SHAPE OF THE PLUNGE POOL.

ABOVE RIGHT THE COURTYARD OF THIS SIXTIES HOUSE BY MARCEL BREUER USES THE CONTEMPLATIVE NATURE OF GRAVEL INSTEAD OF PLANTS. DEEP EAVES WITH LARGE CUT-OUTS ADD SHADE FOR DINING OUTDOORS. THE ANGULAR CHAIR ONE BY KONSTANTIN GRCIC FOR MAGIS ARE USED ALONGSIDE HIGH TECH ARMCHAIRS BY PIERO LISSONI FOR LIVING DIVANI.

RIGHT EVEN THE SMALLEST OF OUTDOOR SPACES BENEFITS FROM A LITTLE BIT OF GREENERY. IN A TINY HOUSE WEDGED BETWEEN TWO BUILDINGS IN PARIS, A TALL STAND OF BAMBOO ACTS AS A WONDERFULLY LEAFY GREEN WALL. WEATHERED TIMBER DECKS AND BENCHES CONTINUE THE NATURAL LOOK.

inside out

WITH A DEEP DECK THAT
EXTENDS THE INTERIOR OUT
INTO THE GARDEN, THIS
OUTDOOR AREA IS FRAMED BY
A SOLID TIMBER BRISE-SOLEIL.
THE TIMBER SOFA USES
OUTDOOR FABRIC FOR THE
SEAT BUT BLURS THE LINE
BETWEEN INSIDE AND OUT
WITH KILIM CUSHIONS.

green zone

KEEPING COOL IN MARRAKECH
IS OF PRIME IMPORTANCE. IN
THIS LUSH COURTYARD THE
MOORISH INFLUENCE IS
EVERYWHERE FROM THE TILES,
TO THE OCTAGONAL FOUNTAIN.
RECLINING DAY BEDS OFFER THE
IDEAL PLACE TO SLEEP OR READ.

A MODERN HOME SURROUNDED BY VICTORIAN TERRACES IN LONDON COMBINES BRIGHT WHITE RENDERED WALLS WITH LIMESTONE PAVERS. THE SLIVER OF WATER AND DRY CLIMATE PLANTS ADD AN EXOTIC FLAVOUR, WHILE THE KONSTANTIN GRCIC CHAIRS FEEL SUITABLY CONTEMPORARY FOR THE SPACE.

ABOVE LEFT VERY FRENCH, THE DELICATE CAST IRON POSTS OF THIS VINE-COVERED TRELLIS DATE FROM THE LATE 19TH CENTURY. PALE GRAVEL AND PAINTED WHITE SHUTTERS ALLOW THE GARDEN TO TAKE ON AN ALMOST TROPICAL LOOK.

ABOVE MAKING FULL USE OF THE LOCAL ABILITIES WITH PLASTERING, THIS ROOFTOP TERRACE HAS DEEP BUILT-IN SEATING TO CATCH BREEZES AND ENJOY THE VIEWS OVER AN OLD DUTCH FORT IN SRI LANKA. BOUGAINVILLEAS ADD COLOUR TO THE TIMBER FRAME THAT SUPPORTS SHADE CLOTHS.

LEFT WITH A MOUNTAIN VIEW LIKE THIS, NOT MUCH MORE IS NEEDED THAN A SHADE CLOTH AND A RUSTIC UPHOLSTERED BENCH. THE CASUAL AIR IS MAINTAINED BY THE RAKISH ANGLE OF THE TIMBER POSTS AND THE SEA OF LOOSE CUSHIONS.

on reflection

ONE OF THE OLDEST TRICKS IN THE DECORATOR'S
HANDBOOK, BUT RARELY USED OUTDOORS, MIRRORED PANELS
MAKE A COURTYARD LOOK MUCH BIGGER THAN IT REALLY IS. THE
CAST IRON FURNITURE FEATURES OLD WORLD NATURE-INSPIRED
MOTIFS IN ACANTHUS LEAVES AND BAMBOO.

in order

THE WHITE WALLS AND UPHOLSTERY PIECES ARE A STRONG
STATEMENT OF ORDER AGAINST THE LUSH TROPICAL FOLIAGE.
SERGIO RODRIGUES SHERIFF CHAIRS IN THE WIDE COVERED
AREA AT RIGHT LINK THE INTERIOR AND EXTERIOR TREATMENT.

vertical volumes

LEFT GROUPED AROUND A FIREPLACE IN A CENTRAL
COURTYARD SUNTRAP, RICHARD SCHULTZ'S CLASSIC
1966 OUTDOOR ARMCHAIRS FOR KNOLL ECHO THE
EXPANSE OF WHITE PAINTED WALLS. THE DELICATE
GREENERY HIGHLIGHTS THE VERTICALITY OF THE
BUILDING AND ITS SIMPLE GEOMETRIC VOLUMES.

monumental scale

RIGHT A SOFT OFF-WHITE STONE FAÇADE
REPLICATES THE COLOUR OF THE TREE TRUNKS
IN THE GARDEN BEYOND. WHITE SEATING SUCH
AS THE CORONA CHAIR BY POUL VOLTHER FOR
ERIK JØRGENSEN HAVE THE SAME SCULPTURAL
QUALITIES AS THE WHITE CERAMIC PLANTERS
ADJACENT TO THE MOSS GARDEN.

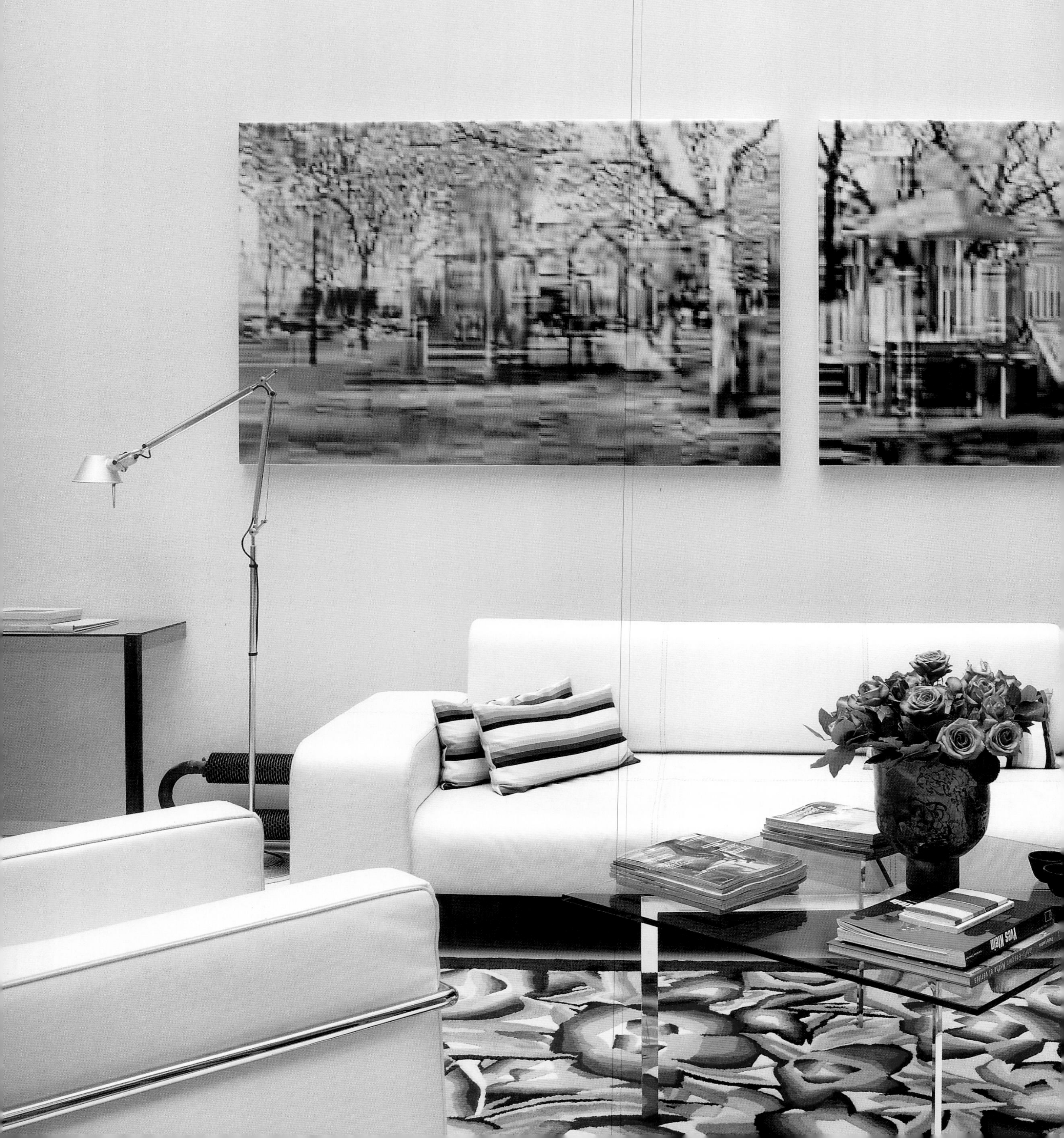
Yves Klein

7

GERARD FAIVRE APARTMENT, PARIS

*Interior designer Gerard Faivre
approaches each project by looking at
its unique relation to the site as well as
its history. The aim is to enhance the
beauty of each space and achieve a perfect
balance of ancient and modern. Here his
skill is applied to his Paris apartment.*

GERARD FAIVRE, THE OWNER AND INTERIOR DESIGNER OF THIS TINY, WELL-LOCATED APARTMENT, has cast something of a modernist spell over an ancient ceramic workshop in Saint-Germain-des-Prés in Paris. He acknowledges the good, 'It opens onto an internal courtyard of a very beautiful Haussmann building from the first half of the 19th century' as well as the bad, 'While the site had been lived in since the war, it had rising damp and the floor remained raw soil.'

Faivre has renovated many buildings in rural and urban sites and has a finely tuned sensibility, so was quickly able to assess that there was natural light which could be exploited, and the existing 35 square metres could be doubled with careful planning, and a little excavation, to assist in the creation of a 30 square metre mezzanine level.

To take advantage of the courtyard, he installed large bay windows, while on the inside he removed doors and increased the amount of integrated storage so that the light could penetrate every room. His goal was to combine aspects of lightness, brightness and functionality. The walls are a soft light white, which not only warms the space but emphasises the contemporary spirit. 20th century engravings and coloured photos are placed horizontally to accentuate the length of the walls and the same effect is achieved with the storage strips that visually elongate the space.

'I also use white to absorb the light,' says Faivre. 'The clarity of white and strong lines are the recipe to enlarge the space, making it full of light yet still restful.'

Faivre plays with a subtle linking of tones. 'For this project, I started using the white from the white leather couch and had the walls painted in the same tone,' he says. 'I often use white to emphasise the colour of an object, painting or a piece of furniture.'

The other key colour which recurs through the apartment is a sharp apple green, seen in the translucent glass of the stairway, the flash of a bathroom stool, and the accessories. All link with the green and white combination found in the courtyard, accentuating the relationship of inside and out.

He injects confidence into the space through the use of pattern, which makes a strong statement considering the rug and the artwork in the living area have the potential to fight, but instead work together well. 'My experience in fashion has helped me to understand colours more,' says Faivre. 'Fashion has taught me to play with colours whilst keeping the elegance and balance.'

He is also a master at incorporating the old with the new, carefully managing all the elements of each project. 'A beautiful old piece is often able to be put in context in a contemporary space,' says Faivre. 'Each site is thought about and decorated with its history in mind. You have to follow its era and adapt current trends without ever forgetting the past.'

FAIVRE HAS EMPLOYED A NUMBER OF DEVICES, INCLUDING HIGHLY FUNCTIONAL LONG, LOW STORAGE STRIPS, TO VISUALLY ENLARGE THE COMPACT APARTMENT.

TO INCREASE THE
FLOW OF LIGHT,
PARTITION WALLS
WERE AVOIDED
AND STREAMLINED
INTEGRATED STORAGE
INTRODUCED. THE
STAIRS APPEAR TO
BE SUSPENDED, WITH
COLOURED GLASS
RAILS ADDING TO
THE TRANSPARENCY
OF THE SPACE.

'To gain even more light, we used white walls and furniture.
We used a few touches of colour carefully spread out so that they
would reflect and warm up the atmosphere of the space.' **Gerard Faivre**

DECORATIVE DETAILS

IT'S IMPORTANT TO REMEMBER WHEN DECORATING that everything, from the macro to the micro, has a role. That includes the structure of the house, the colour and texture of the flooring, the patina of walls, the furniture and, significantly, the smaller objects placed within the space.

While white is a great platform on which to layer other elements, restricting yourself to an all-white palette can be limiting. Bringing in subtle texture and colour through furniture, fabrics, artworks, ceramics and glass adds character, with each new layer affecting everything around it. It really is akin to creating a type of 3-D collage.

The approach depends on your aesthetic, whether it be a case of less is more, do more with less or more always means more. All these approaches to decorating are illustrated, and it is interesting to witness often how successfully styled pieces are grouped for maximum effect. Sometimes it's a supremely confident artwork over a fireplace, a light that becomes a sculpture or a mirror reflecting an ethereal photograph and silvery objects.

White is a blessing for those who favour a multiplicity of objects, allowing a range of shapes, sizes, textures and materials to work together without feeling overwhelming. As a backdrop, it creates a gallery-style setting for the thoughtful arrangement of pieces that may not normally have a relationship. It comes down to how they are placed, noting that the spaces left between them are as important as the space they fill. As stylist Glen Proebstel notes, if you do group together a number of white objects, you can use 'lighting and shadows to create various shapes and forms. Even a minor adjustment, such as moving a ceramic vessel a few inches forward from another, makes working with daylight and shadows more playful.' White cabinetry can be galvanised by the introduction of a few pieces of colour or a densely packed wall of artworks, mementos and objects, while sometimes it is the well-placed timber platter.

Some people can exploit 'It shouldn't work but it does', but for most of us, knowing when to stop isn't easy. In general, it's better to start with a pared-back scheme and introduce one object at a time. Reaching the 'right' balance is something that can be achieved over time. Usually the decorative 'full stop' is evident, but practice really does make perfect.

repeat pattern

THE MATT FINISH ON THESE ORGANICALLY SHAPED
CERAMIC VESSELS FROM ITALIAN MANUFACTURER KOSE
THROW SOFT SHADOWS AGAINST THE SHARPNESS OF
A MIRRORED SURFACE. THE REFLECTION OF THE OBJECTS
IS MADE MORE COMPLEX BY THE MIRROR'S REPEATING
CHEVRON SHAPES.

silver service

SILVER AND WHITE IS A TIME-
HONOURED COMBINATION.
HERE, MIRROR, CRYSTAL AND
SILVER-PLATED OBJECTS ARE
GROUPED ABOVE AN ORNATE
OFF-WHITE MANTELPIECE
RESULTING IN A DELICATE
AND RESTRAINED VIGNETTE.

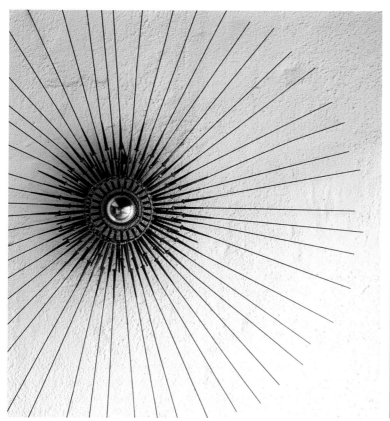

ABOVE COMMONLY REFERRED TO AS A SUNBURST MIRROR, THIS STYLE IS MORE ABOUT AN EXCITING SHAPE AND CREATING VISUAL DEPTH THAN ANY CONCERN FOR OPTICAL ACCURACY. OFTEN INVOLVING A DOMED SURFACE, THE RESULTING DISTORTION MAKES THE MIRROR ALL THE MORE APPEALING.

ABOVE RIGHT THE SOFT MID-TONES OF WOOD ARE SET AGAINST THE HARDNESS OF MARBLE AND GLAZED CERAMIC TILES. TEXTURE COMES FROM BOTH THE NATURAL TIMBER ITEMS AND THE HANDMADE TILES THAT PROVIDE A SUBTLY IRREGULAR SURFACE. THE SPACE IS MADE ALL THE MORE PLEASANT BY DAPPLED NATURAL LIGHT FALLING FROM A HIGH WINDOW.

RIGHT A GROUPING OF MID-CENTURY SWEDISH CERAMICS WITH VERTICALLY INCISED LINES WORKS BEAUTIFULLY AGAINST THE MONOCHROME ARTWORKS IN THE BACKGROUND. VARIETY OF SHAPE AND HEIGHT IS KEY. THE OYSTER WHITE FLOWERS SUPPLY THE CONNECTION FROM EARTHY BROWN TO THE BLACK AND BRIGHT WHITE.

HIGH SHUTTERED WINDOWS ALLOW SOME OF THE OUTDOOR GREENERY TO PERMEATE
INTO THE INTERIOR WHERE MOSS GREEN CUSHIONS ARE JOINED BY OTHERS UPHOLSTERED
IN A COMPLEMENTARY FAWN-COLOURED ANIMAL HIDE. BOTH THESE COLOURS WORK
PERFECTLY WITH THE SOFA'S NATURAL LINEN.

a matter of form

CLASSIC BLACK AND WHITE
IS A DECORATOR'S EASIEST
OPTION. ALWAYS A STRONG
COMBINATION, THE SCHEME
IS ENHANCED HERE BY
A CLEVER MIX OF SHAPES
– WHITE SPHERES IN THE
ARTWORK BY BHAKTI
BAXTER AND A RESTRAINED
FIREPLACE IN BLACK.

THIS PAGE, LEFT THE MARKED CONTRAST BETWEEN DESIGNER OBJECTS AND A CRUMBLING WALL ARE TIED TOGETHER BY A PREDOMINANTLY WHITE GEOMETRIC CABINET BY FRONT FOR PORRO.

THIS PAGE, RIGHT A CLUSTER OF VOLUPTUOUS GLASS OBJECTS ARE REFLECTED IN A LAYERED MIRROR ARRANGEMENT. THE PINK VASE SUCCESSFULLY PICKS UP ON THE COLOUR OF THE STONE MANTELPIECE AND TIES THE DISPLAY TOGETHER.

OPPOSITE PAGE, LEFT ANTIQUE OBJECTS IN SHADES OF WHITE ARE GROUPED TOGETHER IN A DYNAMIC MIX OF SIZE AND SHAPE. THE RESULTING LOOK IS RELAXED AND NATURAL.

OPPOSITE PAGE, RIGHT SET AGAINST A SEA OF WHITE BOOKSHELVES, THE SUBTLE USE OF PASTELS – A PALE BLUE BOOK SPINE AND A PINK SCULPTURAL PIECE BY CERAMICIST MARIA HARTIKAINEN – ADDS A QUIRKY CONTEMPORARY NOTE.

The use of off-white to link rich, sombre browns and reds commonly found in brickwork, velvet curtains and some old marble generally works a treat. This can be contemporised by small doses of pastel colours, such as lemon, pink or pale blue.

JUXTAPOSING EXTREMELY CONTEMPORARY ITEMS, SUCH AS THESE LAMPS, AGAINST
A TRADITIONAL ROOM CAN CREATE A NEW, HIGHLY ARTISTIC VISION. NO LONGER JUST
INTERIOR DESIGN, THE COLLISION OF ERAS CAN BECOME AN ARTWORK IN ITSELF.

in the mix

RATHER THAN STICKING TO
ONE STYLE, IT OFTEN HELPS
TO INTRODUCE A CONTRADICTORY
NOTE. HERE A FORTIES EAMES
CHAIR IS PLACED BESIDE
A DELICATE LACE CURTAIN.
THE RESULT IS A SURPRISINGLY
SOFT AND WHIMSICAL INTERIOR.

ABOVE ONE OF MANY VARIATIONS OF FRISO KRAMER'S REVOLT CHAIR, THIS PARTICULAR EXAMPLE HAS BEEN HAND-PAINTED ON THE SEAT AND BACK. THE CHAIR'S BLACK FRAME HAS A DYNAMIC ANGULAR STANCE AGAINST THE OLD WHITE-PAINTED TIMBER FLOOR.

ABOVE RIGHT GROUPING A SMALL COLLECTION OF MONOCHROME ILLUSTRATIONS – ALL WITH THIN BLACK FRAMES – BESIDE THE BED CREATES A PLEASINGLY GRAPHIC DISPLAY. THE COMBINATION OF TWO SIZES OF RECTANGLE AND A CIRCLE GIVES THE GROUP AN ADDED DYNAMISM, WHILE GREY AND WHITE OBJECTS ARE EASILY ADDED TO THE MIX.

RIGHT A LARGE WHITE EXPANSE BETWEEN ARCHES OFFERS THE OPPORTUNITY FOR A GALLERY-STYLE DISPLAY WITH THE ITEMS ACHIEVING A HEIGHTENED SIGNIFICANCE. HERE, THE FLAT WHITE WALL PROVIDES A CONTRAST TO THE HANDMADE OBJECTS – VINTAGE MOROCCAN POTTERY AND A KORAN HOLDER FROM AFGHANISTAN MOUNTED ON THE WALL.

animal magic

TO HELP THIS SUZANI
UPHOLSTERED PIECE SIT
COMFORTABLY, A MEDLEY
OF HORSE PHOTOS WERE
CHOSEN FOR THE WALL
BEHIND. THE COLOURS
LINK THE TWO AREAS
AND CREATE A
HARMONIOUS BALANCE.

a fine balance

THE TIMBER-PANELLED
DOORS ARE BALANCED
STYLISTICALLY BY THE
FINE BLACK METAL
FRAMES OF MID-
CENTURY FURNITURE
PIECES. THE BLUE
FLOOR WORKS
PARTICULARLY WELL
WITH THE TAN SLING
OF THE HARDOY CHAIR.

GROUPING ARTWORKS IN A VARIETY OF FRAMES TAKES SKILL. HERE, THE SELECTION IS HELD TOGETHER BY THE SIMPLICITY OF WHITE AND A MAJORITY OF THIN BLACK FRAMES RANDOMLY SPREAD THROUGH THE GROUP.

ABOVE LEFT BRIGHT COLOUR LEAPS OUT FROM THE SIMPLE WHITE KITCHEN CABINETRY. THE SMOOTH VACUUM-FORMED HANDLES ARE MUCH LIKE RAYMOND LOEWY'S SIXTIES DRAWER UNITS FOR DOUBINSKY FRERES, BUT THE CANDY COLOURS ARE PURE NINETIES KARIM RASHID.

ABOVE LINKING DIFFERENT OBJECTS IN THE ROOM BY COLOUR IS A STYLIST'S STOCK IN TRADE. HERE, THE BLUE OF THE BARSTOOL IS REPEATED IN THE SMALL OBJECTS ON THE SHELF. ADDITIONAL COLOURS ARE USED, BUT MINIMALLY, ALLOWING THE BLUE TO SET THE COLOUR THEME.

LEFT WHILE ONLY ONE COLOUR IS USED IN THIS GROUP OF OBJECTS, IT'S INTERESTING TO NOTE THAT THE WOVEN RATTAN SHAPE IN THE FOREGROUND AND THE RUSTIC BRICK WALL HAVE A VERY SIMILAR TONE AND SURFACE VARIATION. THIS BALANCES THE BOLD USE OF YELLOW IN A VERY SUBTLE WAY.

unlikely threesome

THREE EXTREMELY DIFFERENT OBJECTS
ARE PLACED IN THE ONE SPACE IN THIS
CLASSIC WHITE PANELLED AND BLACK
FLOORED INTERIOR. THE SERGE MOUILLE
WALL LIGHT HAS AN INDUSTRIAL
QUALITY, THE DRIFTWOOD BENCH AN
ORGANIC ONE, YET THE RED STREET
ART DOLL BRINGS IT ALL TO LIFE.

regarder
sans
désirer

THIS PAGE, LEFT A WALL OF DELICATE ARTWORKS HUNG IN A RIGID FORMATION ARE OFFSET BY A HIGHLY SCULPTURAL SIDEBOARD BY GIO PONTI. TOGETHER, THEY CREATE A LOVELY PLAY ON LINE.

THIS PAGE, RIGHT YELLOW AND GREY ARE A NATURAL PAIRING ENHANCED HERE BY COMPLEMENTARY SHAPES. A LONG THIN WALL-MOUNTED SHELF AND THE SQUARER SHAPE OF THE ARTWORK SITS IN CONTRAST TO SEVERAL CIRCULAR OBJECTS.

OPPOSITE PAGE, LEFT A CHARMING CABINET WITH LINEN-BACKED DOORS PROVIDES THE PERFECT PLACE TO HANG A DELICATE BLACK AND WHITE PHOTOGRAPH. THE MIXED GREYS OF THE CERAMIC VASES DRAW THE ARTWORK AND FURNITURE PIECE TOGETHER.

OPPOSITE PAGE, RIGHT A BRIGHT YELLOW TULIP CHAIR BY PIERRE PAULIN ADDS A HAPPY NOTE TO THIS SUNNY ROOM. PHALAENOPSIS ORCHIDS CONTINUE THE SWEEPING ORGANIC SHAPES.

For those who fear the stark qualities of white, the antidote is timber – in flooring, cabinetry and furniture. Combine with the energy of ochre for a hit of colour that remains within nature's palette.

over easy

THE RIGID RECTANGLES FOUND IN THIS
COLLECTION OF FRAMED ILLUSTRATIONS
BY SANTIAGO RUBINO ARE BALANCED BY
AN EGG-SHAPED EASY CHAIR BY NANNA
DITZEL. THE PARCHMENT WHITE OF THE
ILLUSTRATIONS IS MIRRORED IN THE SOFT
WHITE FABRIC OF THE CHAIR.

playing with shapes

LEFT THE USE OF BERTOIA'S DIAMOND CHAIR IN
THE AIRY OPEN SPACE BRINGS AN OVOID SHAPE
TO THE BOX-STYLE STRUCTURE. WHILE MINIMAL,
THE INTERIOR FEATURES A TILED WALL WITH
DELICATE GEOMETRIC LINES BY BRAZILIAN
ARTIST FABIO FLAKS.

shimmer frame

RIGHT WORKING WITH SIMPLE SQUARE AND
RECTANGULAR RECESSES TO CREATE DEPTH
IN THE WHITE WALL, THE FIREPLACE PROVIDES
A SURPRISE WITH ITS BRILLIANT HAMMERED
GOLD METAL SURFACE TREATMENT BY
GERMAN ARTIST TILLMANN KOEHN.

STUDIO KO CONFESS TO
TAMPERING WITH CONCRETE
'DOSAGE' TO ACHIEVE THE
MILKY CONCRETE FINISH THAT
IS BOTH A COUNTERPOINT TO
THE UNTAMED LANDSCAPE
IN ITS PRECISION AND
COMPLEMENTARY IN
ITS COLOURATION.

8

THIERRY GAUTIER HOUSE, BONNIEUX

Karl Fournier and Olivier Marty of Studio KO had already collaborated with Thierry Gautier on a commercial project for Van Cleef & Arpels in Paris when he approached them to design a holiday house in the Luberon in southern France.

THE CLIENT'S BRIEF WAS QUITE SIMPLE. 'HE WANTED A WEEKEND HOUSE FACING ONLY NATURE,' says Karl Fournier of Studio KO. 'He didn't need a family house but rather an aesthete's or a scholar's loft where he could listen to opera full blast without bothering neighbours. For us it was the nearest thing to a blank page.'

Emphasising this sense of a 'blank page', the architects' first visit to the site was in winter, with 20cm of snow covering the landscape. While the rough shape of the house and the viewpoints were predetermined, the exact orientation came about through the demands of the landscape, the sun's path and the possibility of having extensive views with unadulterated nature in sight. One of the key drivers for the design of the G House, as it is known, was discretion, a contextual approach which was about fitting into the landscape while maintaining a determined modernity.

'The goal wasn't to do a vernacular building that would resemble the local architecture, but rather to understand the surroundings and see how we may echo it,' says Fournier. 'For example, the retaining walls of white stone accentuate the landscape's contour lines, which are nature's architecture.' According to Fournier, nothing equals nature's strength, and therefore white floors and walls are there to pay tribute, and avoid useless rivalry. The same could be said of the pool area with its clear white delineated form sitting within the untamed context of nature.

There are also a series of juxtapositions at play in the house — that of heavy and light, strong and soft, substantial and ephemeral, notably in the treatment of the wall of fabric on the lower floor. 'We wanted to create a sense of levitation as the solidity of the concrete structure seems to defy gravity and float above the fluidity of a white curtain,' says Fournier.

The way in which the local stone walls protect the house and the use of a planted roof ensure it blends with its surroundings, making the house feel discreet. 'Our work always tries to flirt with a certain elegance, while trying to avoid falling into the "showy" trap. For this reason, we prefer a contextual approach, without ever renouncing modernity,' says Fournier.

The interior treatment is typical of Studio KO's skilful mix of flea market finds, custom-made pieces and high-end Moroccan craft. The tactile combination of leather, timber and wool adds warmth to the simplicity and precision of glass, and judiciously used mirrored surfaces. One interior design conundrum was even solved with mirrors.

'We had tried many different installations on the living room wall, and all seemed petty,' says Fournier. 'Nothing compared to the scenery. I recalled advice Andrée Putman had given us during our first encounter in Morocco. She had said, "When something doesn't seem right, and you don't understand why, try to put in a mirror." We applied her philosophy in this case and it worked instantly.' Framed like artworks, the mirrors were placed at an angle to reflect the landscape; yet another indication that Fournier and Marty had no intention of competing with the magnificent surrounds.

EVERYTHING IS GEARED TOWARDS
THE VIEW, AS PIVOTING WINDOWS
OPEN THE HOUSE AND ENGAGE WITH
THE LANDSCAPE. THE INTERIOR IS
FILLED WITH A MIX OF CLASSIC
DESIGN PIECES SUCH AS BRUNO
MATHSSON'S PERNILLA CHAISE
ALONGSIDE PARISIAN FLEA MARKET
FINDS. THE THREE STRATEGICALLY
PLACED FRAMED MIRRORS FURTHER
PULL NATURE INTO THE INTERIOR.

THE CONTROLLED COLOUR PALETTE
OF SOFT GREY AND CREAM IS RICH
IN TEXTURE THROUGH THE USE OF
THE WOOL OTTOMAN AND THE
BENI OURAIN RUG. THE OPACITY
OF THE RODA ARMCHAIRS AND
THE FLUIDITY OF THE CURTAIN
FABRIC ENSURES A LIGHT
DECORATIVE TOUCH.

THE CONTEXT OF THE ROOM, WITH THE WALLS AND POLISHED CONCRETE FLOORS, IS WHITE.
LAYERS OF SOFTNESS ARE ADDED THROUGH THE FABRIC-COVERED BED FROM LIVING DIVANI,
THE RUG AND THE BEDSIDE LIGHT BY VERNER PANTON, ALL IN WHITE. GREYS AND INKY COLOURS
ARE INTRODUCED IN THE CURTAIN FABRIC, THE BEDSPREAD AND THE REMARKABLE TRIPTYCH
BY MANOLO CHRÉTIEN.

FOR THE INTERIOR, THE
ARCHITECTS SOUGHT A 'WHITE
CUBE EFFECT AS IN AN ART
GALLERY', WITH THE IDEA THAT
NATURE IS THE TRUE WORK
OF ART IN THIS INSTANCE AND
EVERYTHING IS GEARED TOWARDS
THE APPRECIATION OF IT.

'*We never use pure white, it is always coloured or warmed up. But whether it is lime, cement or paint, white is omnipresent in our work. It's there to reveal light, or to point out what surrounds it. It brings quietness and serenity into the living space.*' **Karl Fournier**

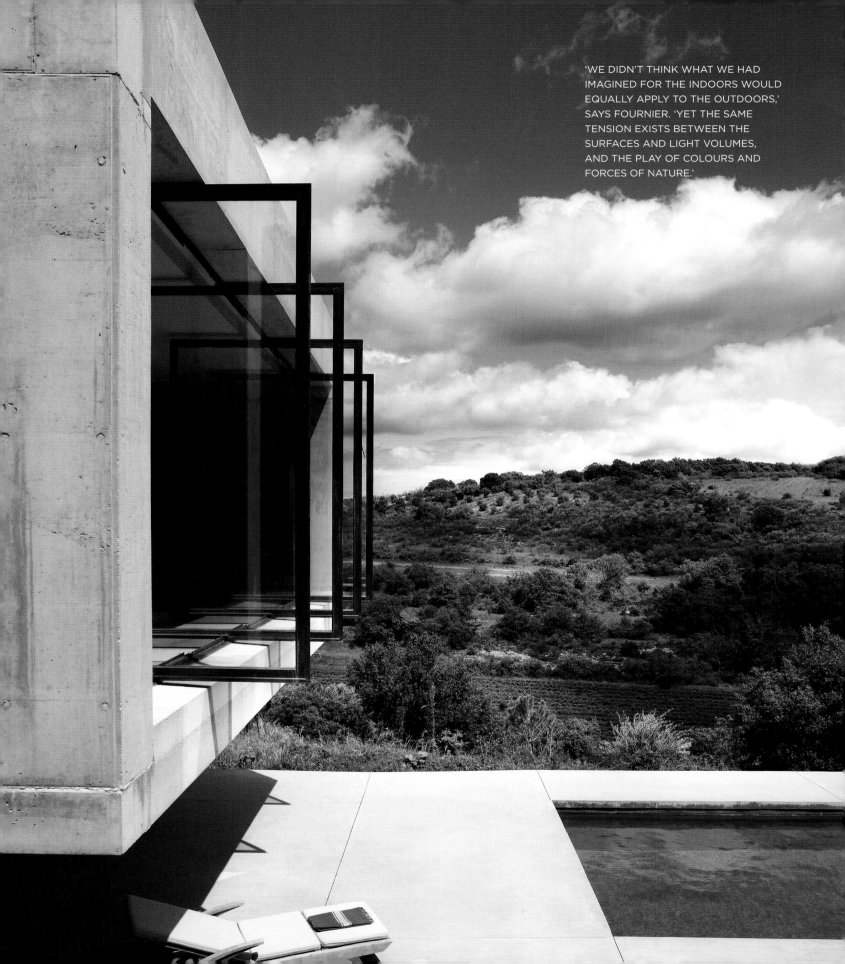

'WE DIDN'T THINK WHAT WE HAD IMAGINED FOR THE INDOORS WOULD EQUALLY APPLY TO THE OUTDOORS,' SAYS FOURNIER. 'YET THE SAME TENSION EXISTS BETWEEN THE SURFACES AND LIGHT VOLUMES, AND THE PLAY OF COLOURS AND FORCES OF NATURE.'

WORKING WITH WHITE

White has so many varied applications in today's homes, from wall and ceiling treatments to floors, collections, fabrics, furniture and outdoor spaces. Here, we share some useful insights and practical tips for working with white across the decorating spectrum.

White-painted boards

While it's not a long-lasting solution, painting
floorboards can work beautifully. Functionally, it's
a compromise, as you tend to see the dust and dirt,
but if you don't mind a casual look with a hint of
dilapidation, then white-painted floors can work
extremely well. Floorboards expand and contract
constantly, so use water-based floor paints as they
move with the timber. Satin is the best sheen level
for floors as it washes almost as well as gloss but
shows less wear.

Referencing an object

For interiors with a lot of objects in the one colour
group, or a dominant coloured item such as a sofa,
it is advisable to think about referencing this colour
in the tinting of the wall and ceiling white. While
this tint will be minuscule, the subtle shade will
work perfectly to become a faint echo of the core
shade. This works irrespective of the central colour
and is universally used to bring the elements of
a room together in a harmonious way.

Indoor-outdoor areas

In the case of a room in which the boundaries between indoors and out have been blurred, paintwork can either reflect a smooth internal finish or offer a more rugged exterior treatment to bring the outside in. The most common types of paint to achieve the latter option are cement-based or limewash. Both are matt and have a subtle but rich texture that signals a link to a garden or outdoor space.

Painting woodwork

Historically, enamel paints used on timber were harder than paints used on walls – this has the practical advantage of making them less prone to wear and easier to clean. The move away from oil-based enamels has seen a rise in popularity of water-based satin finishes which are softer in appearance and more forgiving of imperfections. It's not advisable to use a flatter finish as it tends to show a burnishing mark wherever you attempt to clean it.

Shiny surfaces and white

Sheen level changes your perception of a colour.
When you compare the same colour in flat and
gloss, a different mood is created by each. Flat
paints appear darker because they reflect less
light; putting one sheen level beside another
helps create a sense of dimension. The classic
approach is to take the same colour and use
different sheen levels on various surfaces. If you
play around with that model, you can discover
some interesting effects.

The use of sheer fabrics

One of the most effective additions to a white
space is sheer curtains, particularly in bedrooms
and bathrooms. The diffusion of light provided by
the sheer fabric can create a quite magical glow
and acts like a soft box in a photographer's studio
– reducing hard shadows and making everything
appear warm, smooth and ethereal. Used cleverly
in combination with areas not filtered by fabric,
a wonderful combination of soft and direct light
can be achieved.

A background colour

When you are looking for the right shade of white to act as a background for a collection which incorporates a variety of colours, finishes and materials, raw umber is a great 'one size fits all' tint. It's not yellow, blue or red; instead, it is rather like adding a hint of a timber shade to the white. It has the effect of warming up the white without dominating or fighting with any colour positioned in front of it.

White in open spaces

Large spaces painted brilliant white can often appear cold and uninviting if the white has a blue or black tint – too much of a gallery and not enough of a home. A white open-plan room with large floor-to-ceiling windows can also become blinkingly bright if the house is near water where light reflection is high. To combat this, tints that soften the colour are advised – adding a touch of grey/brown to the paint along with a low-reflection flat wall and ceiling paint is recommended.

Clusters of white

The joy of grouping white objects together is that while they may vary slightly in shade, this only adds to the interest they provide when displayed in a pleasing cluster. Paying particular attention to the shape, materials, height and placement of the objects ensures that, whether they are showcased in front of a dark or a light wall, their form is easily defined. Sculptural objects in white throw shadows that increase the visible 3-D modelling and, as a consequence, enhance the perception of shape.

Gallery white

Popular with galleries worldwide, this particular white is really a non-colour. A white paint without pigments, it is totally neutral and has a flat sheen level so doesn't reflect much light or artificially enhance anything around it. Chosen because it has no impact on the colour and qualities of the artworks, this white can feel a bit clinical in a domestic environment but is well worth considering if the accurate presentation of artworks is of major concern.

Painting outdoor surfaces

While standard acrylic paints are easy to apply, they achieve a predictable result. Look at limewash and cement paints for a softer, more natural feel. While they aren't as washable, and are harder to apply, they are generally unaffected by strong sunlight and last a long time. Limewash has a shorter lifespan in cities as it reacts to acid rain, whereas cement paint will endure and silicate paint will outlast them all. It looks similar to cement paint and has a very low sheen.

Colour and light

Type of light plays a major role in altering the perception of paint tone from room to room, and even from wall to wall. The intensity and colour of light that shines onto paint varies from natural daylight (warm white) to LED (cold white), fluorescent (green) and incandescent light (yellow), making the paint look quite different. Reflected light may also carry a tint with it. A nearby brick wall or a bank of green plants will affect the perceived colour of pale walls around it.

ACKNOWLEDGEMENTS

This book is the result of collaborative effort. Richard Powers' extensive archive of photography was a rich source of material. Design was by Tracy Lines, whose sensitivity to the way images work together to tell a story combines with a beautiful resolution of type. Leta Keens has brought her usual deft touch to the editing.

The support and advice from the team at Penguin/Lantern includes Julie Gibbs, Katrina O'Brien, Emily O'Neill, Hannah Schubert and Evi Oetomo. We thank you all.

Several of the stories were originally sourced by Danielle Miller and Dominic Bradbury, and we are grateful for their sharing.

Without the creativity of the home owners, architects and interior designers who subsequently allowed Richard access to photograph their inspiring spaces, there would be no book.

Geoff Tasker, Director, Murobond Paint, was extremely generous in sharing his lifetime of expertise, and we would also like to thank all the designers and stylists who provided their words of wisdom, including Megan Morton, Fiona Lynch, Thomas Hamel, Sibella Court, Meryl Hare and Glen Proebstel.

Karen & David

PICTURE CREDITS

COVER - Eileen Gray Suite at Riad Mena designed by Romain Michel-Ménière romainmichelmeniere.com riadmenaandbeyond.com

FRONT ENDPAPERS Commune communedesign.com

OPPOSITE TITLE PAGE Pierre Minassian pierre-minassian.fr **OPPOSITE QUOTE** Ben Bischoff made-nyc.com onegirlcookies.com **OPPOSITE CONTENTS** John Rocha johnrocha.ie **3** Popham Design pophamdesign.com **5** Emmanuel Bossuet eemstudio.com

LIVING ROOMS

19 Regis Dho regisdho.com Painting by Emmanuel Meyssonnier **20** Sarah Lavoine sarahlavoine.com Painting by Ara Starck **21 above left** Pierre Frey pierrefrey.com Artwork by Nicolai Howalt and Trine Søndergaard **21 above right** Carol Egan Interiors carolegan.com Artwork by Ghada Amer **21 below right** Ai Wei Wei and HHF Architects hhf.ch Painting by Cai Guo-Qiang **22** Murat Patavi republicaadv.com **23** Justine Brown, Chocolate Brown chocolatebrown.net.au Painting by Justine Brown **24 above left** Fernanda Marques Arquitetos fernandamarques.com.br Artwork by Jonny Detiger **24 above right** Philippe Jousse jousse-entreprise.com Artwork by Andy Warhol **25 above left** Markus Dochantschi/studioMDA studiomda.com **25 above right** Daniel Moynihan colourframe.com **26** Studio Arthur Casas arthurcasas.com **27** David Bentheim *House & Garden* © The Condé Nast Publications Ltd. bentheim.co.uk Artwork by Calder **28 above left** Vipp Styling: Tami Christiansen vipp.com **28 above right** Elodie Sire dmesure.fr Artwork by Desiree Dolron **28 below right** Studio Arthur Casas arthurcasas.com **29** Emmanuel Bossuet eemstudio.com **30** Pierre Yovanovitch pierreyovanovitch.com Artworks by Mark Francis and Franck Scurti **31 above left** Autoban autoban212.com **31 above right** Markus Dochantschi/studioMDA studiomda.com Jonny Detiger jonnydetiger.com **32** Commune communedesign.com **33** Lourenco Gimenes, Forte, Gimenes & Marcondes Ferraz fgmf.com.br Painting by Favio Flacks **34 above left** Studio Catoir studiocatoir.com **34 above right** Isay Weinfeld isayweinfeld.com **34 below left** Pablo Katz Architecture pablokatz-architecture.com **35** Isay Weinfeld isayweinfeld.com **36** Ban Shubber Associates banshubber.com Painting by Suad al-Attar **37 above left** Esther Gutmer and Helena Marczewski esthergutmer.be **37 above right** Carole Katleman Interiors and Dan Cuevas

Artwork by Ugo Rondinone **37 below right** John Friedman Alice Kimm Architects jfak.net **38** Isay Weinfeld isayweinfeld.com **39** Annick Lestrohan, Casa Honoré casahonore.com Artwork by Oignon **40** Daniel Moynihan colourframe.com **41 above left** Martha Bedoya **41 above right** Olivier Renaud-Clément ORC Inc. Steve Blatz blatzarc.com **41 below left** Marcel Breuer restored by Barbara Dente and Donna Cristina dentecristina.com

JOHN ROCHA

47 Photograph by Peter Beard **48** Artwork by John Beattie **49** Artwork by Louis le Brocquy **51** Artworks by Picasso and Guggi

KITCHEN & DINING

55 Studio Guilherme Torres guilhermetorres.com **56** Bade Stageberg Cox bscarchitecture.com **57 above left** Autoban autoban212.com **57 above right** Lourenco Gimenes, Forte, Gimenes & Marcondes Ferraz fgmf.com.br **57 below right** Ben Edwards, Edwards Moore edwardsmoore.com **58** Juan Pablo Rosenberg AR Arquitetos ar-arquitetos.com.br **59** Wonder designofwonder.com.au **60 above left** Sebastian Mariscal Studio sebastianmariscal.com Dominic Bradbury Artwork from Passado Composto Gallery **60 above right** Fernanda Marques Arquitetos fernandamarques.com.br Artworks from Passado Composto Gallery **61 above left** Frank Macchia frankmacchia.com **61 above right** *Elle Decoration Russia* elle.ru/elledecoration **62** Pierre Frey pierrefrey.com **63** Gorka Postigo akaestudio.com **64 above left** Sophie Le Chat sophielechat.fr **64 above right** Stéphane Ghestem, Architecte DPLG abstrakt-architecture.com **64 below right** Isabelle Stanislas so-an.fr **65** Bestor Architecture bestorarchitecture.com Artworks by Kate Eric and Joshua Liberson **66** Chang Architects changarch.com **67** Gerard Faivre gerardfaivreparis.com **68 above left** Arthur Witthoefft andrewmandolene.com **68 above right** Stéphane Ghestem, Architecte DPLG abstrakt-architecture.com **68 below left** Philippe Jousse jousse-entreprise.com **69** Greg Lynn and Jackilin Hah Bloom, Greg Lynn FORM glform.com Artworks by Harold Edgerton **70** UXUS Design uxusdesign.com Painting by Harland Miller **71 above left** KallosTurin Coralie Langston-Jones kallosturin.com Artwork by Zara Hart **71 above right** Kristian Wendelboe and Heidi Volke Painting by Jens Theler **72** Sally Draper sallydraperarchitects.com.au **73 above left** Regis Dho regisdho.com Painting by Emmanuel Meyssonnier **73 above right** Elodie Sire dmesure.fr **73 below left** Victoria Wilmotte victoriawilmotte.fr

BEDROOMS

85 Olivier Renaud-Clément ORC Inc. Steve Blatz blatzarc.com
86 Hudson Architects hudsonarchitects.co.uk **87 above left** Chris Dyson Architects Ltd chrisdyson.co.uk **87 above right** John Friedman Alice Kimm Architects jfak.net **87 below right** Chris Romer-Lee octopi.co.uk Artworks by Pete Seaward and Jenny Ahlner **88** Philippe Jousse jousse-entreprise.com **89** Bestor Architecture bestorarchitecture.com Artwork by Ann Faison **90 above left** Melissa Palazzo, Pal + Smith palandsmith.com Artwork by Rick Meoli **90 above right** Ai Wei Wei and HHF hhf.ch **91 above left** Jakob Blom Painting by Torben Christiansen **91 above right** Heath Ceramics heathceramics.com **92** Josephine Verine Photograph by Li Wei **93** Jean Christophe Aumas, Voici Voila voicivoila.com **94 above left** Wonder designofwonder.com.au **94 above right** Stéphane Ghestem, Architecte DPLG abstrakt-architecture.com **94 below right** *Elle Decoration Russia* elle.ru/elledecoration **95** Elodie Sire dmesure.fr Painting by Jorge Estevez **96** Maryam Montague peacockpavilions.com **97** Rasmus Larrsson design-by-us.com **98 above left** Pierre Frey pierrefrey.com **98 above right** Fontelunga Hotel, Tuscany fontelunga.com **98 below left** KallosTurin kallosturin.com Coralie Langston-Jones **99** Sophie Le Chat sophielechat.fr **100** Jean-Philippe Delhomme jphdelhomme.com **101 above left** Elodie Sire dmesure.fr Artwork by Nick Brandt **101 above right** Annick Lestrohan, Casa Honoré casahonore.com Artwork by Jean Marc Wullsechleger **102** Autoban autoban212.com **103 above left** Carol Egan Interiors carolegan.com **103 above right** Thierry Marx and Mathilde de l'Ecotais mathildedelecotais.com Artwork by Mathilde de l'Ecotais **103 below left** Shim-Sutcliffe Architects shim-sutcliffe.com

BATHROOMS

117 Florence Baudoux Graphic canvas by Floch **118 above left** Emmanuel Bossuet eemstudio.com **118 above right** studio mk27 marciokogan.com.br **118 below left** Isabelle Stanislas **119** Greg Lynn and Jackilin Hah Bloom, Greg Lynn FORM glform.com **120** Stéphane Ghestem, Architecte DPLG abstoprightakt-architecture.com **121** bonetti/kozerski studio LLC bonettikozerski.com Donna Karan International dkny.com **122 above right** Gorka Postigo akaestudio.com **123 above left** Marcelo Ferraz, Brasil Arquitetura brasilarquitetura.com **123 above right** Larson and Paul Architects larsonandpaul.com **124** Annick Lestrohan – Casa Honoré casahonore.com **125 above left** Raquel Silveira **125 above right** Studio Arthur Casas arthurcasas.com **125 below right** Buro Koray Duman burokorayduman.com

126 Studio Guilherme Torres guilhermetorres.com
127 Philippe Jousse jousse-entreprise.com. Painting by Bernard Frize **128** Pierre Yovanovitch pierreyovanovitch.com **129** Geoffrey Dobbs The Dutch House Galle Sri Lanka thedutchhouse.com **130 above left** Antoni Burakowski and Kerry Warn antoniandalison.co.uk **130 above right** Eduardo Longo Arquitetura eduardolongo.com **130 below right** Donovan Hill Architects donovanhill.com.au **131** *Elle Decoration Russia* elle.ru/elledecoration **132** Thorp Design thorp.co.uk **133** Sabrina Bignami b-arch.com **134** Melissa Palazzo of Pal + Smith palandsmith.com Photograph by Billy & Hells **135 above left** Donovan Hill Architects donovanhill.com.au **135 above right** Bestor Architecture bestorarchitecture.com **135 below left** Sharon Fraser Architects Pty Ltd sharonfraserarchitects.com.au **136** Ben Edwards, Edwards Moore edwardsmoore.com **137 above left** Rasmus Larrsson design-by-us.com **137 above right** KallosTurin kallosturin.com Coralie Langston-Jones

STAIRS & HALLS

149 Leeton Pointon leetonpointon.com **150** Fontelunga Hotel, Tuscany fontelunga.com **151 above left** Wonder designofwonder.com.au **151 above right** Vipp Styling by Tami Christiansen vipp.com **151 below right** Greg Lynn and Jackilin Hah Bloom, Greg Lynn FORM glform.com **152** Annick Lestrohan – Casa Honoré casahonore.com **153** Vipp Styling by Tami Christiansen vipp.com **154 above left** Jonathan Adler jonathanadler.com Artwork by Mel Bochner **154 above right** Vipp Styling by Tami Christiansen vipp.com **155 above right** Lourenco Gimenes, Forte, Gimenes & Marcondes Ferraz fgmf.com.br **156** Stéphane Ghestem, Architecte DPLG abstrakt-architecture.com **157** Jacky Mol centimetervoorcentimeter.nl **158 above left** Marcelo Ferraz, Brasil Arquitetura brasilarquitetura.com **158 above right** Marcelo Ferraz, Brasil Arquitetura brasilarquitetura.com **158 below right** Pierre Yovanovitch pierreyovanovitch.com Painting by Stephan Balkenhol **159** Marcelo Ferraz, Brasil Arquitetura brasilarquitetura.com **160** Greg Natale Design gregnatale.com Painting by Judith Johnson **161** Dos Architects *House & Garden* © The Condé Nast Publications Ltd. **162 above left** Brian Zulaikha Tonkin Zulaikha Greer Architects tzg.com.au **162 above right** Diana Kellogg dkarchitects.com Painting by Kathryn Lynch **162 below left** Carol Egan Interiors carolegan.com **163** Maryam Montague peacockpavilions.com **164** Isay Weinfeld isayweinfeld.com **165 above left** Maryam Montague peacockpavilions.com **165 above right** Sacha Walckhoff christian-lacroix.fr

CHRIS DYSON

168 Artwork by Martin Richman

OUTDOOR SPACES

177 Rachel Zoe rachelzoe.com **178** Sabrina Bignami b-arch.it
179 above left Annick Lestrohan – Casa Honoré casahonore.
com **179 above right** UXUS Design uxusdesign.com
179 below right Alexandre Herchcovitch herchcovitch.com.br
180 Annick Lestrohan – Casa Honoré casahonore.com
181 Esther Gutmer and Helena Marczewski esthergutmer.be
182 above left Lourenco Gimenes, Forte, Gimenes &
Marcondes Ferraz fgmf.com.br **182 above right** Kerry Hill
Architects kerryhillarchitects.com **183 above left** Carole
Katleman Interiors **183 above right** Pablo Katz Architecture
pablokatz-architecture.com **184** Barton Myers Associates, Inc.
bartonmyers.com **185** KallosTurin kallosturin.com
186 above left John Friedman Alice Kimm Architects jfak.net
186 above right Marcel Breuer restored by Barbara Dente
and Donna Cristina dentecristina.com **186 below right**
Stephane Parmentier stephaneparmentier.com **187** Studio
Arthur Casas arthurcasas.com **188** Daniel Moynihan
colourframe.com **189** Tim Gledstone squireandpartners.com
190 above left Elodie Sire dmesure.fr **190 below left**
Kasbah Bab Ourika kasbahbabourika.com **191** XTEN
Architecture xtenarchitecture.com randolphduke.com
192 Isay Weinfeld isayweinfeld.com **193 above left**
David Jameson Architect davidjamesonarchitect.com
193 above right Frank Macchia frankmacchia.com

GERARD FAIVRE

194 Artworks by Olaf Rauh **197** Artwork by Prassinos
200 Artwork by Baraud Parage

DECORATIVE DETAILS

203 Studio Catoir studiocatoir.com **204** *Elle Decoration Russia*
elle.ru/elledecoration Photograph by Philippe Assalit
205 above left Commune communedesign.com **205 above
right** Wonder designofwonder.com.au **205 below right**
Artwork by Juan Gatti **206** Fontelunga Hotel, Tuscany
fontelunga.com **207** Carole Katleman Interiors and Dan Cuevas
208 above left *Elle Decoration Russia* elle.ru/elledecoration
208 above right Martha Bedoya Mirror by Martha Bedoya **209
above left** Chris Dyson Architects Ltd chrisdyson.co.uk **209
above right** Sophie Le Chat sophielechat.fr Ceramics by Marta
Hartikainen **210** Isabelle Stanislas so-an.fr **211** Brinkworth Dinos
Chapman and Tiphaine de Lussy brinkworth.co.uk **212 above
left** UXUS Design uxusdesign.com **212 above right** Stéphane
Parmentier stephaneparmentier.com Drawings by Mrzyk &
Moriceau at Air de Paris Gallery **212 below right** Maryam
Montague peacockpavilions.com **213** Elodie Sire dmesure.fr
Photographs by Aline Coquelle **214** Sophie Le Chat
sophielechat.fr **215** Sacha Walckhoff christian-lacroix.fr
Artworks by Jean Cocteau, Antoine Tempé, Stephane Fretz,
Christian Lacroix, Georges Barbier, Thomas Boog, Mathieu
Mercier (Galerie Chez Valentin), Hans Bellmer, Erteé, Hella
Jongerius (Galerie Kreo), Suzanne Ramié for Madoura
216 above left Greg Lynn and Jackilin Hah Bloom, Greg Lynn
FORM glform.com **216 above righ**t Victoria Wilmotte
victoriawilmotte.fr **216 below left** Annick Lestrohan – Casa
Honoré casahonore.com **217** Isabelle Stanislas so-an.fr
218 above left George Yabu and Glenn Pushelberg
yabupushelberg.com Artworks by Ewan McDonald
218 above right Lourenco Gimenes, Forte, Gimenes &
Marcondes Ferraz fgmf.com.br Artwork by Cildo Meireles
219 above left Carol Egan Interiors carolegan.com Photograph
by Chris Honeysett **219 above right** Mark Dixon Architect
markdixonarchitect.com **220** George Yabu and Glenn
Pushelberg yabupushelberg.com **221 above left** Lourenco
Gimenes, Forte, Gimenes & Marcondes Ferraz fgmf.com.br
221 above right Tillmann Koehn *House & Garden* © The Condé
Nast Publications Ltd. tillmannkoehn.com

& WORKING WITH WHITE

236 Hamilton Design Associates hdanyc.com Painting by
Andrew Taylor **238 above left** Chris Romer-Lee octopi.co.uk
238 above right Martha Bedoya **239 above left** Studio
Guilherme Torres guilhermetorres.com **239 above right**
Wonder designofwonder.com.au **240 above left** Markus
Dochantschi/studioMDA studiomda.com Painting by Jonny
Detiger jonnydetiger.com **240 above right** Martha Bedoya
241 above right George Yabu and Glenn Pushelberg
yabupushelberg.com **242 above left** Barbara Rourke
allthebellsandwhistles.com **242 above right** John Rocha
johnrocha.ie **243 above left** John Rocha johnrocha.ie
243 above right Sharon Fraser Architects **244** Florence
Baudoux Artwork by Benjamin Sabatier **246** KallosTurin
kallosturin.com **251** KallosTurin kallosturin.com **253** George
Yabu and Glenn Pushelberg yabupushelberg.com

BACK ENDPAPERS Ban Shubber Associates banshubber.com

CASE STUDIES

#1 Lázaro Rosa-Violán lazarorosaviolan.com

#2 John Rocha johnrocha.ie

#3 Erica Tanov ericatanov.com

#4 Eduardo Longo Arquitetura eduardolongo.com

#5 Susan Fraser facebook.com/pages/House-in-Lherm-France/194207347397072

#6 Studio KO studioko.fr

#7 Chris Dyson Architects Ltd chrisdyson.co.uk

#8 Gerard Faivre gerardfaivreparis.com

Every attempt has been made to trace the owners of copyright materials, but in some cases this has proved impossible. The authors and publisher will be glad to receive information leading to more complete acknowledgements in subsequent printings of the book and in the meantime extend their apologies for any omissions.

LANTERN

UK | USA | Canada | Ireland | Australia
India | New Zealand | South Africa | China

Penguin Books is part of the Penguin Random House group of companies whose addresses can be found at global.penguinrandomhouse.com.

Penguin
Random House
Australia

First published by Penguin Group (Australia), 2015

10 9 8 7 6 5 4 3 2 1

Text copyright © Karen McCartney and David Harrison 2015
Photographs copyright © Richard Powers 2015

The moral right of the authors has been asserted.

Cover and text design by Tracy Lines @ TLC
© Penguin Group (Australia)
Typeset in Mrs Eaves by Tracy Lines
Colour separation by Splitting Image Colour Studio, Clayton, Victoria
Printed and bound in China by Toppan Leefung Printing Ltd

National Library of Australia Cataloguing-in-Publication data:

Creator: McCartney, Karen, author.
White rooms: Decorating with style, pattern and colour /
Karen McCartney, David Harrison; photography by
Richard Powers.
ISBN 9781921383793 (hardback)
Subjects: Colour in interior decoration.
Interior decoration.
Other Creators/Contributors
Harrison, David, 1963- author.
Powers, Richard, photographer.

747.94

penguin.com.au/lantern

Karen McCartney has a wealth of experience in the areas of interior design, art and architecture. From an Honours degree in the History of Art & English from University College London, and her first job on British magazine *Art Monthly*, Karen has written for British *Elle Decoration*, *The Financial Times* and *The World of Interiors*.

In Australia she edited *Marie Claire Lifestyle* and was founding editor of interiors magazine *Inside Out*, a position she held for 10 years. She has written three books on the subject of residential architecture – *50/60/70 Iconic Australian Houses* and a sequel *70/80/90 Iconic Australian Houses* – both of which formed the basis of a successful national touring exhibition launched at the Museum of Sydney in 2014. *Superhouse: architecture and interiors beyond the everyday*, published by Penguin/Lantern, looks at prevailing themes in residential architecture, globally.

White Rooms is her first collaboration with husband David Harrison, and her second with photographer Richard Powers.

David Harrison, a Sydney-based design journalist and stylist, has been contributing to Australian interiors magazines since 1999 and has seen his work published in numerous titles including *Belle*, *Vogue Living*, *Real Living*, *Inside Out*, *Habitus*, *Design Quarterly* and *The Weekend Australian* magazine. He also contributes to Indesignlive and the Powerhouse Museum's D*Hub blog.

After many years reporting on the Milan Furniture Fair, he developed the Design Daily blog (designdaily.com.au) where he posts on global and local design trends. It is subscribed to by design aficionados worldwide.

In this book he brings his knowledge of design detail, how spaces work, the way furniture and artworks contribute to the success of a space and the practical aspects of working with white interiors.

Richard Powers began his photographic career in 1991 with a series of books called 'Cultures of the World', covering El Salvador, Nicaragua, Dominican Republic, Syria and Denmark. By 1996, his interests in design and architecture saw him diversify to incorporate interiors and still life into his repertoire. Based in London, he began shooting for publications such as UK *Elle Decoration*, *House & Garden*, *The Sunday Times* and *The Telegraph*. Emigrating to Australia he spent seven years shooting for local and international titles worldwide as well as campaign shoots for Australian Tourism and advertising agencies.

Richard has continued to expand his interior and architecture portfolio as well as an array of still life, lifestyle and travel images. He is regularly commissioned and submits for many titles worldwide including *AD*, *Elle Décor*, *WSJ*, *The World of Interiors*, *Vogue Living*, *AD* Spain, France, Russia, China as well as many of the *Elle Decoration* titles

He has 13 books to his name, including *The Iconic House* and *Mountain Modern*, both by Dominic Bradbury, and *Superhouse* by Karen McCartney. Richard's personal portfolio can be viewed at www.richardpowers.co.uk